THE GR

BARBECUE

COOKBOOK

THE GREEN

BARBECUE

COOKBOOK

MODERN VEGETARIAN GRILL AND BBQ RECIPES

MARTIN NORDIN

Hardie Grant

BOOKS

INTRODUCTION

I have always loved to barbecue, but only more recently – in the last few years – I have realised the opportunities I have been missing in terms of textures. For me, the joy of the barbecue lies in the taste, as the charcoal, wood and smoke bring so much to the dish. I've realised, though, that not only does cooking over fire allow for more complex flavours, but it also allows for a contrast of textures.

This realisation has helped me to create more contrast in the food I make. I use a lot of vegetables in my cooking, and I treat them in different ways in order to create interest in the dish. It could be to mix it for an emulsion sauce, to fry it until it is crispy, or to cook it until it is incredibly soft.

When thinking about grilling burgers, I was struck by how liberating and creative it is to devise, prepare and eat green burgers. A classic meat-based burger is indeed uncompromisingly classic, but what goes into a green burger is far less restrictive. There's not one classic, so you have free rein! Do what you want, experiment and question what a burger can be. You have the freedom to just go for it. I want to inspire you to have the courage to try out different variants, so you can then start to create your own favourite.

Another thing I love about barbecues is the process of cooking over the fire. It is a more welcoming way to cook like this, rather than standing over a technical induction hub in a cramped kitchen. It allows you to gather around the fire and to invite people to come and cook together.

My friends have inspired me a lot in my cooking. We often do big dinners, where we all cook together. Over time, more and more friends started becoming vegetarian so the food became more plant-based. Gradually, over a couple of years, we turned it from vegetarians bringing their extra protein to the dinners, to the meat eaters having to bring their meat, if they wanted any. Then, with time, I found so many ways of doing great things with vegetables – it just felt like there were no boundaries so I could be more creative.

I began to find I had so much inspiration and ideas to try out. Then, with the added push of social media, my cooking went from a hobby to something that took up more of my time and focus. It has got to the point that now most of my professional and personal time revolves around food.

For this book, I want you to initially try following the recipes, with the idea that you can use them to be inspired to create your own dishes. Next time you might combine it with another recipe or even think of another idea inspired by something delicious you ate in your favourite restaurant or something you saw when searching the web. Remember, too, that not everything depends on the food – the social dimension of gathering, cooking food together and hanging out around the fire is also a wonderful experience.

But not everything depends on the food – the social dimension of gathering, cooking food together and hanging out around the fire is a wonderful experience.

Grilling vegetables

When I began barbecuing vegetables I followed my gut instinct a lot of the time. Did the flames seem hot? Were the vegetables taking on a good colour and did they smell good? Did the grill sound right – did the vegetables sizzle when I added them? That's probably most people's approach to the process of grilling on the barbecue and you can go far with it. But to ensure a higher degree of certainty that you will achieve the desired results for your raw ingredients, it is well worth giving a little extra thought to which type of barbecue and charcoal you want to use, as well as the temperature of both the grill and the ingredients themselves.

I usually use a barbecue with a lid (preferably with a thermometer). You need the lid when grilling indirectly, because the grill becomes your oven. Sometimes, I also use a tabletop barbecue. It is common in parts of Asia and is perfect if you want to barbecue together with friends – everyone can gather around it at the table. Of course, you can also grill straight over an open fire. For a larger party, a fun idea is to saw a metal barrel in half lengthways and use it as a barbecue. Be creative – but always remember fire safety!

Vegetables are generally more sensitive than meat when being grilled. The fuel you choose can have an impact on the flavour both positively and negatively. I usually use charcoal, which offers several advantages. Charcoal is more precise than wood and is better suited to barbecuing using a grill when you want to achieve the most even spread of heat possible. Additionally, it burns for longer and smokes less, which helps to better preserve the original flavour of your raw ingredients.

On the other hand, if you want to add another flavour dimension, you should barbecue using wood. Since this smokes far more than charcoal, it can contribute a variety of smoky flavours to whatever you are barbecuing. It also feels much cooler to use wood! It burns, it's fragrant and it looks more real - the way you want fire to look! I like to use woods like apple and cherry – fruit trees generally – as well as woods like oak. However, I often end up using birch since it is cheaper and easier to get hold of.

I rarely use briquettes, but they are also fine to use. Regardless of the fuel you choose to use, it is important to ensure that they are FSC certified, as this ensures that the wood is free from chemicals and has been grown sustainably. It's good for you and the environment.

Once you have chosen your fuel, it's time to light the barbecue. Never use lighter fluid – ignite it using a chimney starter or an electric charcoal lighter. Then all you have to do is place the vegetable straight into the flames or just after they have died down if you are going to charcoal roast it. Otherwise, wait for the perfect glow if you are going to grill it more carefully. How do you know what the best glow is? When is it perfect? That depends on what you want to do – are you caramelising an onion straight over the glow or perhaps roasting a swede using indirect heat? The charcoal is at its best – and hottest – when it is glowing and has a grey, ash-like exterior. During the next phase, when the charcoal has turned white, the temperature has begun to fall and it is often slightly too late to start grilling. A simple (and unscientific) method for checking the temperature is the hand trick. Hold your hand about 10 cm (4 in) above the glowing coals. If you can only keep your hand there for 1 second, it's very hot – more than 300°C (575°F). If you can keep your hand there for 2 seconds, it's around 200–250°C (400–480°F), 3–4 seconds means the temperature is 175–200°C (350–400°F), and if you manage 5–7 seconds then it is less than 150°C (300°F).

Consider the core temperature

You might think it sounds strange to check the core temperature of a vegetable, but you probably wouldn't bat an eyelid if it was meat or fish. Try to find the vegetable's densest or 'meatiest' part and take the temperature there. One important thing to bear in mind when measuring the temperature is that there is a big difference between something like a fresh summer cabbage that will cook quicker than a stored winter harvest that needs longer to finish – so do keep track! It goes without saying that the texture varies greatly depending on season, growing conditions, weather and much more.

A rule of thumb is that the greater the density of your vegetable, the higher the core temperature should be when it is cooked. A potato should ideally exceed 95°C (200°F), whereas courgettes (zucchini) or asparagus are at their best at 75°C (170°F). But, of course, it varies depending on how the vegetable is going to be used: a leek can be perfect with a core temperature of around 80°C (175°F) if you want it *al dente* in a salad, but if you want to eat it by digging out the contents using a spoon, like in the recipe on page 108, it needs to be over 95°C (200°F). The same rule applies to the aubergine (eggplant) if it is being made into baba ghanoush – the whole idea is for the aubergine (eggplant) flesh to be cooked to a pulp in its skin. Make a habit of checking the core temperature of everything you grill so that you have a benchmark to use the next time you are making the same recipe. If you don't have a thermometer, you can use a needle tester to see how soft the insides of your vegetables are.

Cooking without a barbecue

Cooking vegetables over an open fire is unbeatable when it comes to producing deep flavours, but don't forget that you can go far using your regular cooker. Add grill stripes using a griddle pan and use the oven to finish off your vegetables. You won't have the same, wonderful barbecue flavour, but the principles of cooking are effectively the same.

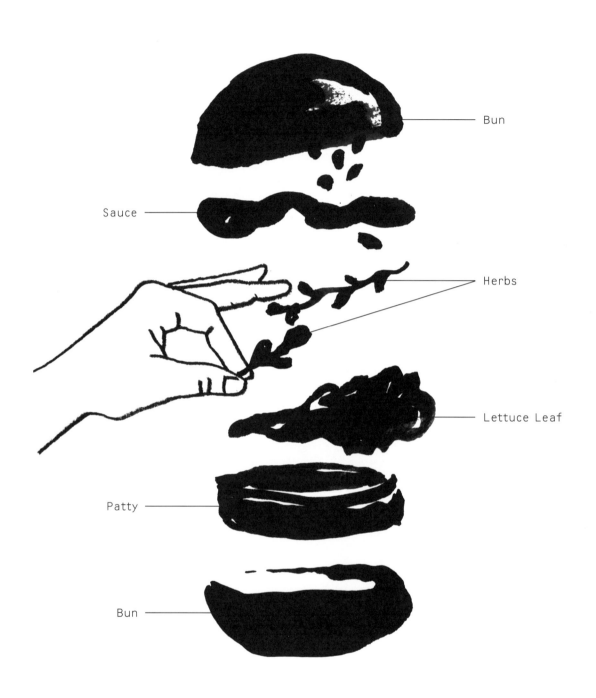

Bun

Sauce

Herbs

Lettuce Leaf

Patty

Bun

STRUCTURE OF A BURGER

Many of the burger recipes in this book are inspired by dishes that I've eaten and that have seemed ideal for deconstructing and reconstructing between two slices of bread. Just as with all cooking, the secret to creating a wicked burger is achieving the perfect combination of textures and flavours. It's all about balance. If the patty is deep-fried and crispy maybe you'll need something acidic to counterbalance the greasy taste. If part of the burger seems on the dry side — for example, if the patty is based on legumes — maybe some mayonnaise would even things out.

The patty

Most patties improve if they're left to rest in the refrigerator for a few hours before you cook them. It's a good idea to prepare bean patties the evening before, and then cook them for supper the day after. Patties for deep-frying are best if you freeze them first.

Lettuce leaves and other greens

Forget everything you've heard about lettuce always having to be at the bottom of the burger – totally immaterial if you ask me. For my part, I think there's often a bit too much of an emphasis on lettuce – there are, after all, quite a lot of other greens that work well in burgers.

The bun

I've used several different buns for the burgers on pages 32–61, and you'll find a couple of my favourites on pages 192–195. The choice of bun should be based on the flavour of the patty. A slightly sweeter brioche bun goes excellently with a salty bean patty, whilst a patty made of Jerusalem artichokes — which are slightly sweet — would maybe go better with a crispy bun based on poolish (a kind of starter). Or just leave out the bun entirely and serve the patty in a lettuce leaf instead.

The sauce

If the recipe includes mayonnaise, ketchup, a herb sauce or a creamy miso sauce, this is to contribute juiciness or counterbalance acidity. I usually serve the sauce on the side, so everyone can add it according to their own taste.

Herbs

Do sprinkle on plenty of herbs – maybe even instead of lettuce leaves. Is the herb in flower? Make use of that! Most herb flowers are edible and create a further dimension – both flavour-wise and visually.

MAKING THE JOB EASIER

You can easily go over the top with special utensils, but there are good ones that I simply find it hard to do without when I'm cooking.

Knife: A good (and nice-looking!) knife. Keep it sharp and, whatever you do, always wash it by hand!

Food ring: A food ring is unbeatable for shaping perfect bean patties, and it also helps hold together patties that would otherwise easily spread over the frying pan (skillet). Buy food rings in different sizes so you can adjust the patty size to the bun size.

Grater: Invest in a really good grater for small jobs such as grating lemon zest, cheese or truffles. I've tried out several makes, but nothing beats the Microplane.

Digital scales: Sometimes, such as when baking, you simply need more precise weights, and that's where digital scales come in.

Digital thermometer: There's a huge range on the market, but many of them are absolutely useless. Loads of thermometers have packed up on me, so invest in a really good one. Essential for deep-frying, but also good for checking that the vegetables are cooked through.

Wooden spoon: For scraping up stuff that otherwise easily sticks to the bottom of the saucepan, a wooden spoon is unbeatable.

Salad spinner: Good for removing liquid from beans or getting lettuce crispy after an ice bath.

Slotted spoon: Essential for deep-frying – for pushing round, turning and lifting things out.

Flat griddle pan: Cooking bean patties on a grill can be tricky – they easily get stuck, and after a while half the burger will have fallen through the bars. Buy a flat griddle pan and brush the patties generously with some oil – problem solved!

Spatula: Handy when you want to get that little bit more out of the bowl.

Mandoline: To get really thin slices and julienne strips. For me, it's nearly as important as a good knife.

Kitchen tweezers: For twirling up potato strips, lifting a sage leaf out of the fryer or just removing something. You never know when you'll need them, so have them close at hand.

Washing-up brush: Having things clean and ship-shape on the draining board and washing up as you go are at least as important as having all the ingredients in place when you start off.

01

BARBECUE STRAIGHT ON THE GRILL

GRILLED CAULIFLOWER with gremolata

Serves 6

2 cauliflower heads

100 ml (3½ fl oz/scant ½ cup) rapeseed
    (canola) oil

150 g (5 oz/⅔ cup) unsalted butter

salt

Gremolata

6 tablespoons finely chopped parsley leaves

2 tablespoons pine nuts, toasted

1 tablespoon finely chopped green chilli

1 tablespoon finely chopped garlic

1 unwaxed lemon, finely zested

sea salt flakes

To serve

90 g (3½ oz) whitecurrants

1   Light the barbecue (grill) and let the charcoal take on a strong, even glow. Prepare a package to cook the cauliflower in by putting a slightly smaller sheet of baking parchment on top of a slightly larger sheet of kitchen foil. Keep close to hand.

2   Mix all the ingredients for the gremolata in a bowl.

3   Slice each cauliflower head into three 'steaks'. Cut from the root end so that you have a piece of root attached to each slice. Lightly brush both sides of each slice with oil.

4   Grill the pieces of cauliflower so that they take on some grill marks. Place them on the baking parchment, cover with the butter and season with salt. Fold the package together to create a sealed parcel and place it back on the barbecue – preferably in a position that is less hot – and close the lid.

5   Open the package after about 30 minutes and check that the cauliflower has turned a beautiful shade of golden-brown and is starting to soften. The florets should flex if you press them gently. Take the temperature of the root – when it is around 80°C (180°F), the cauliflower is ready.

6   Place one slice of cauliflower on each plate, dollop a large tablespoon of gremolata onto each slice and top with the whitecurrants.

BOOST THE FLAVOUR **Use the parsley stalks in the gremolata – chop them as small as you can. This delivers a delicious, deep, slightly bitter parsley flavour, which compliments the other flavours in this dish nicely.**

GRILLED CORN with creamy pecorino sauce

Serves 6

6 corn cobs in their husks

150 g (5 oz/⅔ cup) unsalted butter,
    at room temperature

2 garlic cloves, finely chopped

sea salt flakes

Lemon oil

shaved peel of ½ unwaxed lemon

100 ml (3½ fl oz/scant ½ cup) rapeseed
    (canola) oil

Pecorino sauce

2 shallots, finely chopped

2 tablespoons unsalted butter

1 tablespoon white wine vinegar

200 ml (7 fl oz/scant 1 cup) whipped cream

200 g (7 oz) grated (shredded) pecorino
    or alternative hard sheep's cheese

To serve

Fermented Tree Onions (page 210) or garlic cloves

1. Bring a large saucepan of lightly salted water to the boil.

2. Fold down the leaves on the corn and remove any threads between the leaves and corn. Place the cobs in the water with the tips facing down and boil for around 5 minutes. Remove the corn from the pan and fold the leaves back around the cobs.

3. Mix the butter and garlic in a bowl using a fork. Set aside.

4. Heat the lemon peel and oil in a small saucepan. Remove the pan from the heat when it starts to simmer and leave to stand for around 10 minutes so that the oil takes on the flavour of the lemon. Remove the lemon skin from the oil and set aside.

5. Fry the shallots in the butter on a low heat so that they soften but do not start to brown then add the vinegar. Continue stirring until the shallots have absorbed the vinegar. Mix in the cream and cook for another 3 minutes. Using a hand-held blender or food processor, blend the sauce until smooth and stir in the grated cheese. Season with salt.

6. Light the barbecue (grill). Place the corn on the barbecue while the charcoal is still burning. If you prefer, you can put them straight onto the burning charcoal. Grill the corn until the leaves are almost completely black – they act as a protective cover on the corn.

7. Remove the corn from the barbecue, fold down the leaves and spread the corn with the garlic butter.

8. Spoon a little of the sauce onto a plate and place a cob on top. Drizzle with lemon oil and top with some chopped Fermented Tree Onions or garlic cloves. Repeat with the remaining cobs.

GRILLED PEAS AND SPRING ONIONS
with mint and bean sprouts

Serves 6

12 small spring onions (scallions)

3 tablespoons olive oil

1 kg (2 lb 4 oz) peas in pods

125 g (4 oz) bean sprouts

10 g (½ oz) chopped mint leaves

sea salt flakes

1 Light the barbecue (grill) and let the charcoal take on a soft glow.

2 Split the spring onions lengthways – try to keep some of the leaves. Brush the cut edges of the spring onions with oil. Place the spring onions on the barbecue and leave them until they have taken on some colour and started to soften – this should take around 10 minutes. Turn them over and grill on the other side for around 5 minutes. Place the spring onions in a large bowl and set aside.

3 Place the peas in their pods on the barbecue and leave them until the pods start to blacken – this should take around 5 minutes. Turn them over and leave for a further 5 minutes. Remove from the barbecue and allow them to cool. When the pods are cool enough to handle remove the peas from the pods and place the peas in the bowl with the spring onions.

4 Drizzle the remainder of the oil into the bowl, then add the bean sprouts and mint. Stir so that everything is airy – ideally using your hands – and season with salt. Place onto a large plate and serve as a side dish or a starter.

SHIITAKE with whisky and miso-marinade

Serves 6

600 g (1 lb 5 oz) shiitake

Whisky and miso marinade

4 tablespoons whisky, preferably Balvenie
    or another Speyside or Japanese whisky

4 tablespoons rapeseed (canola) oil

2 tablespoons dark miso

2 tablespoons tamari

juice of ½ lime

1 tablespoon cane sugar

1 garlic clove

1 teaspoon sesame oil

To serve

6 egg yolks

1 tablespoon thyme leaves

sea salt flakes

cornflower petals (optional)

1 Mix together all the ingredients for the marinade using a hand-held blender or food processor.

2 Clean the mushrooms and cut them into 3–4 mm (⅛ in) thick slices. Place them on a sheet of baking parchment and brush with the marinade. Turn them over and brush the other side.

3 Light the charcoal in the barbecue (grill) and let it take on a fine, soft glow. Grill the mushrooms on the barbecue, turning them over occasionally and brushing them with a little more marinade. Once the mushrooms take on a nice, caramelised golden-brown colour, they are done.

4 Plate up the mushrooms. Place an egg yolk in the middle of the plate and top with thyme, sea salt flakes and some cornflower petals, if you have some to hand.

BEER-MARINATED AUBERGINE with tomato sauce and shiitake tossed in butter

Serves 6

Beer-marinated aubergine

3 large aubergines (eggplants)

330 ml (11¼ fl oz/1⅓ cups) beer, e.g. brown ale

2 garlic cloves, lightly crushed

2 tablespoons malt vinegar

2 teaspoons salt

Tomato sauce

6 large tomatoes

2 tablespoons olive oil

2 small yellow onions, finely chopped

1 tablespoon tomato purée (paste)

1 tablespoon white wine vinegar

1 tablespoon powdered sea buckthorn

100 ml (3½ fl oz/scant ½ cup) mushroom stock

salt (optional)

Shiitake tossed in butter

2 tablespoons rapeseed (canola) oil

300 g (10½ oz) shiitake

2 tablespoons unsalted butter

1 tablespoon whisky, preferably Balvenie
  from Speyside (optional)

salt

To serve

2–3 sprigs of coriander (cilantro)

1   Cut the aubergine into slices 1–1½ cm (½ in) thick. Mix the rest of the ingredients for the marinade together in a plastic bag then add the slices of aubergine. Rub the aubergine through the bag so that the marinade is evenly distributed. Leave to rest in the refrigerator for 7–8 hours. Take it out a few times and rub the aubergine or shake the bag to ensure the aubergine is evenly coated in the marinade.

2   Halve the tomatoes then coarsely grate them into a bowl. Once you have finished grating, you should only have the tomato skin left in your hand.

3   Add the olive oil to a frying pan (skillet) on a medium heat and gently brown the onions. Add the tomato purée and raise the temperature slightly. Stir with a wooden spoon for around 5 minutes so that the tomato purée takes on a more intense, darker colour. Add the vinegar, powdered sea buckthorn, mushroom stock and the grated tomatoes. Reduce the heat, add salt to taste, and leave to simmer for 20–30 minutes. Strain the tomato sauce so that it is smooth – I usually use a sieve (fine-mesh strainer).

4   Light the charcoal in the barbecue (grill) and let it take on a steady, fine glow. Take the aubergine slices out of the marinade. Place them on paper towels and blot the cut edges until dry. Grill the aubergine slices until they turn a deep colour and have a crust.

5   Heat the rapeseed oil in a frying pan and wait until it is smoking. Add the mushrooms and fry them until they begin to colour. Lower the heat slightly and add the butter. Stir to ensure that the mushrooms are covered in the butter, and season with salt. I usually add some whisky when frying mushrooms, so add a tablespoon or so if you have any. Continue frying for a few more minutes and then set the mushrooms aside.

6   Serve either on a plate or in a bowl. Pour out a little tomato sauce, place the aubergine slices in the sauce and top with the mushrooms and coriander.

GRILLED ASPARAGUS with burrata, egg yolk and kumquat sauce

Serves 6

1 kg (2 lb 4 oz) asparagus

2 tablespoons rapeseed (canola) oil

Kumquat sauce

12 kumquats, sliced

2 tablespoons grated turmeric

1 vanilla pod (bean), split lengthways

3 star anise

100 ml (3½ fl oz/scant ½ cup) honey

300 ml (10 fl oz/1¼ cups) water

To serve

6 burrata balls

6 egg yolks

6 tablespoons Roasted Buckwheat (page 206)

chive flowers (or another onion flower)

6 teaspoons Leek Ash (page 96)

1   Light the barbecue (grill) and let the charcoal take on a fine glow.

2   Make the kumquat sauce. Bring all the ingredients to the boil in a saucepan on a high heat. Boil for around 10 minutes until it begins to thicken and is foaming a lot. Strain the sauce into a bowl through a sieve (fine-mesh strainer) and press as much of the kumquat fruit through as possible.

3   Trim and wash the asparagus. Ideally, peel them all the way to the top – you don't have to, but it looks good! Dry them and place in a bowl together with the rapeseed oil. Mix so that they are covered in the oil then place the asparagus on the barbecue. Roll them back and forth constantly for around 5 minutes, taking care to ensure they don't burn too much. Remove them from the grill once they have blacked slightly.

4   Take a burrata ball and tear it in half using your hands. Place it on a plate and let the cream drain out. Place a pile of asparagus beside it, put an egg yolk on the burrata and cut into it so that the yolk runs out. Drizzle with 3–4 tablespoons of kumquat sauce. Top with Roasted Buckwheat, Chive Flowers and Leek Ash.

GRILL THE STALKS **The stalks of chive flowers and onion flowers are almost inedible when raw - they're hard and wooden. But if you grill them, they're great to eat and offer a lovely onion tone.**

MEZCAL with grilled grapefruit

Serves 6

6 ruby grapefruit (about 600 ml/20 fl oz/2½ cups)

12 tablespoons cane sugar

60 ml (2 fl oz/¼ cup) beetroot (beet) juice

360 ml (12 fl oz/1½ cups) mezcal (or a
	smoky tequila)

600 ml (20 fl oz/2½ cups) club soda

1 Light the barbecue (grill). Halve the grapefruit. Pour a tablespoon of sugar onto each cut edge and press it in with your fingers. Wait a few minutes to allow the sugar to dissolve into the juice. Place the grapefruit halves onto the barbecue, cut-side down, directly above the charcoal. Ideally, there should be flames so that the sugar and pulp char slightly.

2 Using a citrus reamer, press the juice out of the charred grapefruit into a mixing bowl. Add the beetroot juice and mezcal, and mix.

3 Prepare the drinking glasses. Add the ice and then divide the mixture equally between the glasses. Top with 100 ml (3½ fl oz/scant ½ cup) club soda, mix gently and serve.

GARNISH LIKE A PRO **Why not garnish with a piece of the grilled grapefruit? All you have to do is cut a small slice off the grilled part before squeezing out the juice.**

BLACK BEAN AND KING OYSTER BURGER

Serves 6

rapeseed (canola) oil or peanut oil, for frying

60 g (2 oz) finely chopped yellow onion

1 teaspoon Tabasco, or Midsummer's Louisiana
   Hot Sauce (page 207)

3 tablespoons HP sauce or other brown sauce
   (steak sauce)

2 large king oysters

50 g (2 oz) walnuts, peeled and chopped

mild chilli powder, e.g. piment d'Espelette

sea salt flakes

150 g (5 oz/2½ cups) cooked black beans

2 tablespoons finely chopped parsley leaves

40 g (1½ oz/scant ½ cup) cooked beluga lentils

300 g (10½ oz/3⅓ cups) cooked porridge
   (oatmeal)

To serve

2–3 red (bell) peppers

1 tablespoon olive oil

6 burger buns, halved

1 tablespoon unsalted butter

6 eggs

6 tablespoons mayonnaise

parsley leaves

1   Heat some rapeseed oil in a frying pan (skillet) and fry the onions on a fairly high heat until they have browned thoroughly and are almost on the verge of being burnt. Lower the heat, mix in the Tabasco and HP sauce and take the frying pan off the heat.

2   Cut the mushrooms into ½ cm (¼ in) cubes. Warm plenty of oil in a frying pan on medium heat. Add the mushrooms and fry until soft, for around 20 minutes. Drain the oil.

3   Toast the walnuts in a dry cast-iron pan on a medium heat until they begin to colour, for around 2 minutes. Shake the pan occasionally to make sure the nuts don't burn too much. However, it doesn't matter if they take on a lot of colour. Remove the pan from the heat and season with chilli and salt.

4   Place the walnuts in a bowl together with the beans, parsley, lentils, porridge, mushrooms and a pinch of salt. Mix together using a potato masher (the beans should only be slightly mashed). Add the onion mixture and stir to ensure that everything is mixed.

5   Shape the batter into six round patties – either by hand or by using a food ring. Place them on a plate and cover with cling film (plastic wrap). Leave them to stand in the refrigerator for at least 1 hour – preferably longer – so that they hold together better when being grilled.

6   Light the barbecue (grill) and grill the peppers until they turn black on the outside. I usually place the peppers onto the barbecue while the fire is still burning – preferably on top of a wood-burning fire. Put the peppers in a plastic bag and leave to cool for around 10 minutes. Rub the skin off by massaging the peppers while they are still in the bag. Cut into even strips.

7   Heat a few tablespoons of olive oil in a cast-iron pan, either on the hob or on the barbecue. Fry the patties on a medium heat for a few minutes on each side. Then place them on the barbecue in indirect heat, close the lid and roast for 10–15 minutes.

8   Brush the cut surface of the buns with olive oil and grill them quickly on the barbecue.

9   Wipe out the cast-iron pan, then add in a tablespoon of butter. Return it to the grill and fry the eggs.

10 Add a generous tablespoon of mayonnaise to each bun and place the burger on top. Top with the grilled pepper, parsley and the fried egg.

COURGETTE AND MUNG BEAN BURGER
with Sriracha mayonnaise and furikake

Serves 6

200 g (7 oz) yellow onions, finely chopped

2 tablespoons rapeseed (canola) oil

150 g (5 oz/⅔ cup) cooked rice

200 g (7 oz) courgette (zucchini)

300 g (10½ oz) mung beans, cooked

50 g (2 oz/scant ½ cup) buckwheat flour

1 tablespoon Korean dried red pepper

1 tablespoon sesame seeds

1 teaspoon virgin coconut oil

1 teaspoon toasted sesame oil

1 pinch of Chinese five spice

To serve

6 burger buns, halved

unsalted butter

salad leaves

spring onions (scallions), finely chopped

bean sprouts

6 tablespoons Sriracha ayonnaise (page 202)

6 teaspoons Furikake (page 206)

1 Place the onions in a cold saucepan together with a tablespoon of the rapeseed oil. Put the saucepan on a medium heat and cover with a lid. The onions will quickly start to release moisture and by letting them cook in their liquid, the flavour will be concentrated. Stir using a wooden spoon every 5 minutes until completely soft.

2 Add the onions and rice to a food processor and pulse until smooth.

3 Cut the courgette into thin batons. Place them in a bowl together with the onion and rice mix and the rest of the ingredients. Mix together using a wooden spoon or your hands (the beans should only be slightly mashed).

4 Heat a frying pan (skillet) and add the remaining tablespoon of rapeseed oil. Lift a little batter at a time into the frying pan using a large spoon and shape into small patties. Fry for around 1 minute on each side so that they take on a little colour. If you like, you can use a shaper at the very beginning to make sure the patties retain their shape better. Place the shaper into the frying pan and fill with the batter. When cooked, place the patties on a baking sheet and leave to cool. Cover with cling film (plastic wrap) and leave in the refrigerator for at least 1 hour so that they set.

5 Light the barbecue (grill) and let the charcoal take on a strong, even glow. Butter the buns on the cut surface and grill them quickly on the barbecue. Then quickly grill the patties on either side so that they warm up and get an even crispier surface.

6 Add a few salad leaves to each bun and place a patty on top. Add the spring onions, bean sprouts, plus a tablespoon of Sriracha Mayonnaise and top with the Furikake.

HARISSA-MARINATED AUBERGINE
BURGER with baba ghanoush and dukkah

Serves 6

2 medium aubergines (eggplants),
    about 600 g (1 lb 5 oz)

Harissa marinade

4 tablespoons rapeseed (canola) oil

2 tablespoons Harissa (page 207)

1 pinch of ground cumin

juice of 1 lime

1 tablespoon cane sugar

1 garlic clove

Baba ghanoush

2 medium aubergines (eggplants),
    about 600 g (1 lb 5 oz)

2 garlic cloves, with the skin on

juice of ½ lemon

1 teaspoon mild chilli powder, e.g. piment
    d'Espelette

100 ml (3½ fl oz/scant ½ cup) olive oil + a little
    extra for serving

sea salt flakes

To serve

6 burger buns, halved

1 tablespoon olive oil

1 unwaxed lime, finely zested

Dukkah (page 204)

1 Mix all the marinade ingredients together using a hand-held blender or food processor.

2 Cut the aubergines into slices 1 cm (½ in) thick. Pour the Harissa marinade into a plastic bag and add the aubergine slices. Rub the aubergine through the bag so the marinade is evenly distributed. Leave to rest in the refrigerator for 7–8 hours. Take it out a few times and rub the aubergine or shake the bag to ensure it is evenly coated.

3 Light the charcoal in the barbecue (grill). Continue making the baba ghanoush. Pierce the aubergines in a few places using a cocktail stick (toothpick) and then place them straight onto the glowing charcoal in the barbecue, even if the charcoal is still burning. Grill the aubergines until the skin has charred completely and the aubergine is soft inside, around 15 minutes. Add the garlic when there is 5–10 minutes left and grill them until they are also soft inside. Set the garlic and aubergine aside until they are cool enough to handle.

4 Cut the aubergines lengthways and remove the flesh with a spoon (try to remove as much flesh as possible). Halve the garlic and scoop out the flesh. Place the garlic and aubergine flesh into a large mixing bowl. Add the lemon juice, chilli powder and a little olive oil, and mix using a whisk. Add the rest of the oil, a little at a time, while mixing vigorously. If you prefer a firmer consistency, reduce the amount of oil used. Season with salt.

5 Remove the aubergine slices from the marinade, place them on paper towels and dry the cut edges. Add the aubergine slices to wooden skewers and grill on the barbecue. Turn them occasionally and brush with a little more marinade. Once the aubergines start to take on a nice, caramelised golden-brown colour, they are done. Set aside and brush again with the marinade.

6 Brush the buns with olive oil on the cut surface and grill them quickly on the barbecue.

7 Add 2–3 slices of aubergine to each bun, dollop 2 generous tablespoons of baba ghanoush on top, grate some lime zest over and top with Dukkah.

BLACK BEAN BURGER
WITH CHEDDAR AND CARAMELISED ONIONS

Serves 6

400 g (14 oz/2½ cups) cooked black beans

rapeseed or peanut oil for frying

65 g (2¼ oz/scant ½ cup) finely chopped onion

1 teaspoon mild chilli powder, e.g. piment
   d'Espelette

1 teaspoon smoked paprika

3 tablespoons BBQ sauce

50 g (2 oz/scant ½ cup) Dry-Roasted Walnuts
   (page 220)

2 tablespoons finely chopped coriander (cilantro)

100 g (3½ oz/scant ½ cup) boiled black rice

25 g (1 oz/scant ½ cup) panko breadcrumbs

sea salt

Caramelised onions

2 onions

2 tablespoons butter

1 tablespoon red wine vinegar

To serve

120 g (4 oz) Cheddar

6 burger buns, halved

butter for the buns

cos lettuce leaves (romaine)

1. Rinse the beans in cold water and drain in a colander.

2. Heat a little oil in a frying pan (skillet) and fry the onions over a fairly high heat until they have taken on colour and are on the verge of burning.

3. Reduce the heat, add the chilli and paprika powders and stir. Stir in the BBQ sauce and take the frying pan off the heat.

4. Roast the walnuts as described on page 220.

5. Chop the walnuts and put them in a bowl together with the beans, coriander, rice, panko breadcrumbs and a pinch of salt. Mix the ingredients together with a potato masher (the beans should only be lightly mashed). Add the onion mixture and stir so that everything is well combined.

6. Take a handful of mixture at a time and shape into 6 round patties, either by hand or using a food ring (page 12). Put the patties on a large plate and cover with cling film (plastic wrap). Put in the refrigerator for at least an hour, preferably longer, so that they will hold together better when you fry them.

7. Peel and chop the onions and put them into a cold saucepan. Add the butter and put the saucepan over a medium heat, and then put the lid on. The onions will soon start to release liquid, and the flavours will be concentrated as a result of their cooking in their own juices. Stir with a wooden spoon about once every 5 minutes until completely soft, and check they are not burning. (If you notice they're starting to get dry you can add the vinegar earlier.)

8. Remove the lid, pour over the vinegar, raise the heat and cook for about 15 minutes, stirring, until considerably reduced. Set aside.

9. Preheat the oven to 180°C (350°F/Gas 4).

10. Heat a few tablespoons of the oil in a frying pan over a medium heat. Fry the patties for a few minutes on both sides until they have developed a nice colour. Transfer them to an ovenproof dish. Put a few slices of cheese on each patty, place in the oven and leave until the cheese has melted.

11. Butter the buns on the cut surface and fry them quickly in a frying pan or grill (broil) them in the oven.

12. Place a patty on the bottom of each bun. Put a cos lettuce leaf on top and slap on a generous spoonful of the caramelised onion.

GRILLED AVOCADO BURGER with marinated beans and crème fraîche

Serves 6

3–4 medium avocados
juice of 1 lime
olive oil

Marinated beans

200 g (7 oz/1¼ cups) cooked black beans
2–3 Smoked Tomatoes (page 208)
1 spring onion (scallion), finely chopped
1 teaspoon finely chopped serrano chilli
1 tablespoon finely chopped coriander (cilantro)
1 teaspoon finely chopped garlic
1 tablespoon white wine vinegar
2 tablespoons olive oil
zest of 1 lime

To serve

6 burger buns , halved
butter for the buns
6 tablespoons crème fraîche
parsley and coriander (cilantro)
cayenne pepper

1. Rinse the beans and drain them well in a colander.
2. Light the barbecue and make the Smoked Tomatoes on page 208. You can use unsmoked tomatoes, but the smoky flavour adds a fantastic dimension to the bean mixture. Chop 2–3 tomatoes and mix them and the other ingredients with the marinated beans in a bowl. Stir carefully and put to one side.
3. Halve the avocados and remove the stones, then carefully scoop out the avocado flesh with a spoon. Cut slices that are as big as possible – about 1 cm (½ in) thick, depending on the size of the avocado. Put the slices on a plate and brush them first with lime juice and then with oil.
4. Grill the avocado slices quickly on the barbecue over a really high heat or burn off the surface with a blowtorch. The surface of the avocado should be caramelised, nearly burnt, while the inside should be cold and retain its consistency.
5. Butter the buns on the cut surface and grill (broil) them quickly on the barbecue.
6. Slap a generous dollop of marinated beans on each bun. Then add 2 slices of avocado, a dollop of crème fraîche and a little parsley and coriander. Finish off by sprinkling over a pinch of cayenne pepper.

QUINOA AND SWEET POTATO BURGER
with horseradish sour cream, shallots and chives

Serves 6

3 medium sweet potatoes, about 600 g (1 lb 5 oz)

2 eggs

100 g (3½ oz/scant 1 cup) chickpea (besan) flour

1 teaspoon chilli powder, preferably piment
    d'Espelette

1 tablespoon wholegrain Dijon mustard

1 tablespoon Walnut Butter or other Nut Butter
    (page 220)

juice of ½ lemon

1 pinch of sea salt

200 g (7 oz/1 cup) quinoa

rapeseed or peanut oil, for frying

Horseradish sour cream

3 tablespoon finely grated horseradish

300 g (10½ oz/1¼ cups) sour cream

sea salt

To serve

6 burger buns, halved

butter for the buns

finely sliced red Asian shallots

finely chopped chives

1 Preheat the oven to 200°C (400°F/Gas 6).

2 Put the sweet potatoes into an ovenproof dish and bake them in the middle of the oven for about 45 minutes or until they are soft all the way through.

3 Split the potatoes lengthways and scoop out the insides with a spoon.

4 Lightly whisk the eggs in a food processor using a knife blade. Add the sweet potatoes, chickpea flour, chilli powder, mustard, Nut Butter, lemon juice and salt, and pulse-blend until all the ingredients are well combined. Transfer to a bowl and add the quinoa. Turn the mixture with a spoon so that everything is well blended.

5 Take a handful of mixture at a time and shape into 6 round patties, either by hand or using a food ring (page 12). Put the patties on a plate and cover with cling film (plastic wrap). Put in the refrigerator for at least an hour, preferably longer, so that the patties will hold together better when you fry them.

6 Preheat the oven to 180°C (350°F/Gas 4).

7 Mix the horseradish and sour cream in a bowl. Add salt to taste and put to one side.

8 Heat a few tablespoons of oil in a frying pan (skillet). Fry both sides of the patties for a few minutes over a medium heat, until they have developed a little colour. Transfer to an ovenproof dish and bake them in the middle of the oven for 5–10 minutes.

9 Butter the buns on the cut surface and fry them quickly in a frying pan or grill (broil) them in the oven.

10 Put a patty at the bottom of each bun, splash on some horseradish sour cream and top with shallots and chives.

OVEN-BAKED JERUSALEM ARTICHOKE
BURGER with creamy miso sauce and herb mix

Serves 6

1 kg (2 lb 3 oz) Jerusalem artichokes (sunchokes)

rapeseed or peanut oil, for frying

6 tablespoons butter

Herb mix

2 tablespoons finely chopped rosemary

2 tablespoons finely chopped thyme

6 tablespoons finely chopped parsley

2 teaspoons crushed green peppercorns

2 teaspoons white wine vinegar

2 tablespoons olive oil

sea salt

Miso sauce

50 g (2 oz/¼ cup) butter

4 tablespoons miso paste

300 ml (10 fl oz/1¼ cups) pouring
  (whipping) cream

To serve

6 burger buns, halved

butter for the buns

lettuce leaves

1   Preheat the oven to 200°C (400°F/Gas 6).

2   Mix all the ingredients for the herb mix in a bowl (the mix will be tastiest if you finely chop the herbs instead of mixing them in a blender).

3   Brush the Jerusalem artichokes clean, but retain as much of the skins as possible. I usually use a hard toothbrush to get into all the nooks and crannies. I also cut away the small knotted parts, where there can be a lot of soil.

4   Heat the oil in a frying pan (skillet) until it starts to smoke. Fry the Jerusalem artichokes until the skins are golden brown all over – this takes 10–15 minutes. Transfer the artichokes to a baking tray lined with baking parchment and put in the oven for 10 minutes. Remove from the oven and allow to cool until the artichokes are cool enough to handle.

5   Melt the butter for the miso sauce over a medium heat. Stir in the miso paste. Reduce the heat and whisk in the cream, a little at a time, until you have a glossy, golden brown sauce. Put to one side.

6   Gently bash the Jerusalem artichokes with a spoon so they open up a little. Shape 6 small patties, either by hand or using a food ring (page 12). Put a knob of butter on each patty. Bake in the oven for a further 10 minutes.

7   Butter the buns on the cut surface and fry them quickly in a frying pan or grill (broil) them in the oven.

8   Put a lettuce leaf at the bottom of each bun. Place a patty on top, spoon over a little miso sauce and finish off with a dash of herb mix.

WHITE BEAN BURGER with smoked tomatoes, deep-fried sage and roasted pine nuts

Serves 6

3 onions

2 tablespoons butter

150 ml (5 fl oz/⅔ cup) white wine

750 g (1 lb 10 oz/4 cups) cooked large white beans

50 g (2 oz/scant 1 cup) panko breadcrumbs

1 tablespoons mayonnaise

2 tablespoons Cashew Nut Butter
   or other Nut Butter (page 220)

2 eggs

Deep-fried sage

12 sage leaves

peanut oil, for frying

To serve

18 Smoked Tomatoes (page 208)

6 burger buns, halved

butter for the buns

cos (romaine) lettuce leaves

2 tablespoons toasted pine nuts

1 Preheat the oven to 180°C (350°F/Gas 4).

2 Peel and finely chop the onions. Put them in a saucepan with the butter over a medium heat and fry until the onions are soft. Pour over the wine, raise the heat and cook, stirring, until considerably reduced.

3 Rinse the beans in water and drain in a colander.

4 Mix the beans in a food processor or using a hand blender (they should retain a little structure). Put the beans, the reduced onion mixture and the other ingredients for the patties in a bowl. Stir so that everything is well combined.

5 Take a handful of mixture at a time and shape into 6 round patties, either by hand or using a food ring (page 12). Put the burgers in the refrigerator for at least an hour, preferably longer, so they hold their shape when fried.

6 Pour plenty of oil into a frying pan (skillet), so it reaches 5 mm–1 cm (¼–½ in) up the edge. Heat the oil to 180°C (355°F) and deep-fry the sage until it takes on a deep green colour (making sure it doesn't burn). Remove it and drain it on some paper towel.

7 Pour off a little oil from the frying pan, reduce the heat to medium and fry the patties for a few minutes on both sides until they have developed a golden colour and a crispy surface. Transfer them to an ovenproof dish and bake in the oven for 5–10 minutes.

8 Heat the Smoked Tomatoes in the same frying pan in which you fried the burgers. Pour on a little more oil if necessary. Put to one side and keep warm.

9 Butter the buns on the cut surface and fry them quickly in a frying pan or grill (broil) them in the oven.

10 Put lettuce leaf at the bottom of each bun, and top it with a patty, some tomatoes and deep-fried sage leaves. Finish by sprinkling over some toasted pine nuts.

ROASTING THE PINE NUTS **in a dry frying pan brings out the requisite flavour more clearly. But watch out for rancid nuts, which can give rise to so-called pine mouth – a bitter aftertaste that can ruin your sense of taste for several days.**

CHICKPEA AND GRILLED PEPPER BURGER WITH DILL-DUNKED CUCUMBER SALAD

Serves 6

3 red (bell) peppers

olive oil

sea salt and freshly ground black pepper

200 g (7 oz) Oven-Baked Onions (page 216)

500 g (1 lb 2 oz/3 cups) cooked chickpeas
    (garbanzos)

3 garlic cloves

2 eggs

1 tablespoon smoked paprika

1 tablespoon mild chilli powder, e.g. piment
    d'Espelette

50 g (2 oz/scant 1 cup) panko breadcrumbs

rapeseed or peanut oil, for frying

Cucumber salad

1 bunch of dill

2 cucumbers

zest of 1 lemon

sesame seeds

olive oil

sea salt and freshly ground black pepper

To serve

6 burger buns, halved

butter for the buns

a few dill heads as necessary

1 Preheat the grill (broiler) to 250°C (475°F/Gas 7).

2 Halve the peppers and remove the core and seeds. Put the pepper halves on a baking tray with the skins facing up and drizzle with the oil. Sprinkle with salt and black pepper. Grill (broil) until the skin is black. Remove the peppers and transfer to a plastic bag. Allow them to cool, then rub or pull off the skin and cut into pieces.

3 Make the Oven-Baked Onions (page 216).

4 Rinse the chickpeas in cold water and drain them well in a colander.

5 Peel and finely chop the garlic cloves. Lightly whisk the eggs in a food processor. Add the Oven-Baked Onions, chickpeas, grilled peppers, paprika, chilli powder, panko bread-crumbs, garlic and salt. Pulse-blend so all the ingredients are well combined, but not too finely blended.

6 Take a handful of mixture at a time and shape into 6 round patties, either by hand or using a food ring (page 12). Put the patties in the refrigerator for at least an hour, preferably longer, so that they hold together better when you fry them.

7 Preheat the oven to 180°C (350°F/Gas 4).

8 Take some sprigs of dill for the cucumber salad. Shave the cucumber for the salad lengthways using a vegetable peeler. If you want you can first remove the seeds from the middle – the cucumber will release less water. Put the cucumber shavings in a bowl and mix in the dill, lemon zest, sesame seeds and some dill heads. Drizzle over a little olive oil and carefully turn the salad using your hands. (Avoid using any implements, otherwise the cucumber may get squeezed to pieces.) Season to taste.

9 Heat a frying pan (skillet) over a medium heat and pour in a little oil. Fry the patties for a few minutes on both sides, until they have a nice colour and a crispy surface. Transfer the patties to an ovenproof dish and bake for 5–10 minutes.

10 Butter the buns on the cut surface and fry them quickly in a frying pan or grill them in the oven.

11 Put a patty at the bottom of each bun and top with the cucumber salad, and a few dill heads, as you like.

PEA BURGER with cream cheese mix and king oyster crisps

Serves 6

200 g (7 oz) Oven-Baked Onions (page 216)

30 g (1 oz) mint leaves +

15 g (½ oz) lovage leaves

2 large or 3 medium eggs

50 g (2 oz/scant 1 cup) panko breadcrumbs

800 g (1 lb 12 oz) peas (cooked and cooled,
    or thawed frozen ones)

4 garlic cloves

4 spring onions (scallions)

rapeseed or peanut oil, for frying

Cream cheese mix

120 g (4 oz) cream cheese

2 tablespoons finely chopped garlic

sea salt and pink pepper

King oyster crisps

2–3 king oysters (eryngii)

1 litre (34 fl oz/4 cups) peanut or other
    deep-frying oil

sea salt

To serve

6 burger buns, halved

butter for the buns

crushed pink peppercorns

mint leaves

1 Make the Oven-Baked Onions (page 216).

2 Put the Oven-Baked Onions, mint and lovage in a food processor and mix until everything is finely distributed. Add the eggs and panko breadcrumbs and mix until well combined. Finally, add the peas and pulse-blend or mix quickly for a few seconds so the peas break up a little.

3 Peel the garlic. Finely chop the garlic and spring onions and stir them into the pea mixture.

4 Take a handful of mixture at a time and shape into 6 round patties, either by hand or using a food ring (page 12). Put the patties on a plate and cover with cling film (plastic wrap). Put in the refrigerator for at least an hour, preferably longer, so that they will hold together better when you fry them.

5 Preheat the oven to 180°C (350°F/Gas 4).

6 Mix the cream cheese with the garlic in a bowl. Add salt and pink pepper to taste.

7 For the crisps, thinly slice the mushrooms. Heat the oil to about 180°C (355°F) in a high-sided saucepan. Add the slices of mushroom and deep-fry them until they are golden brown, pushing them around with a slotted spoon. Remove the mushroom crisps and drain on paper towel. Sprinkle with salt on both sides.

8 Heat a few tablespoons of oil in a frying pan (skillet). Fry the patties over a medium heat for a few minutes on both sides, until they have developed a nice colour. Transfer them to an ovenproof dish and bake in the oven for about 5–10 minutes.

9 Butter the buns on the cut surface and fry them quickly in a frying pan or grill (broil) them in the oven.

10 Place a patty on the bottom of each bun. Put a generous dollop of cream cheese mix and some oyster mushroom crisps on top, finishing off with mint leaves and a little crushed pink pepper.

BBQ PORTOBELLO BURGER
WITH CARAMELISED ONIONS AND SAINT AGUR CHEESE

Serves 6

4 Grilled and Steamed Spring Onions
   (page 220)
600 g (1 lb 5 oz) portobello
rapeseed or peanut oil, for frying
2 finely chopped garlic cloves
1 tablespoon butter
100 g (3½ oz) day-old sourdough bread,
   finely chopped
300 ml (10 fl oz) BBQ sauce
2 eggs

Caramelised onions

2 onions
2 tablespoons butter
1 tablespoon red wine vinegar

To serve

120 g (4 oz) Saint Agur or other creamy
   blue cheese
6 burger buns, halved
butter for the buns
finely chopped chives, preferably
   garlic chives with flowers

1. Grill and steam the spring onions as described on page 220.

2. Cut the mushrooms into 5 mm (¼ in) cubes. Heat the oil in a frying pan (skillet) over a high heat until it starts to smoke. Add the mushrooms and fry them so that they take on colour, for 10–15 minutes.

3. Chop the steamed spring onions and add them and the garlic to the mushrooms in the pan. Add the butter, reduce the heat to medium and cook for a few minutes, stirring.

4. Remove the frying pan from the heat and allow it to cool a little. Then add the bread, BBQ sauce and eggs. Stir so that everything is well combined.

5. Take a handful of mixture at a time and shape into 6 round patties, either by hand or using a food ring (page 12). Put the patties in the refrigerator for at least an hour, preferably longer, then they will hold together better when you fry them.

6. Peel and chop the onions for the caramelised onion mix. Put the chopped onions and the butter into a cold saucepan. Cook over a medium heat and put the lid on. The onions will soon start to release liquid, and the flavours will be concentrated as a result of their cooking in their own juices. Stir with a wooden spoon about once every 5 minutes for 30–40 minutes, and check that they are not burning. (If you notice they're starting to get too dry you can add the vinegar earlier.)

7. Add the vinegar, increase the heat and cook for about 15 minutes, stirring, until considerably reduced. Put to one side.

8. Preheat the oven to 180°C (350°F/Gas 4) using the grill function.

9. Heat up a few tablespoons of oil in a frying pan over a medium heat. Fry the patties for a few minutes on both sides, until they develop a nice colour and a crispy surface. Transfer to an ovenproof dish and grill in the oven for 5–10 minutes.

10. Put a little cheese on each patty and cook for a little longer under the grill, until the cheese has melted. This won't take long, so keep an eye on them!

11. Butter the buns on the cut surface and fry them quickly in a frying pan or grill them in the oven.

12. Place a patty on the bottom of each bun. Splash on a heaped spoonful of the caramelised onions and top with chives.

ROASTED CELERIAC BURGER *with herb* cream and chanterelles

Serves 6

3 small celeriacs (celery roots), the diameter
　　should correspond to the size of the bun
rapeseed or peanut oil, for frying
sea salt and freshly ground black pepper

Herb cream

1 bunch of mixed herbs, e.g. thyme,
　　rosemary and dill
juice of ½ lemon
3 tablespoons olive oil
sea salt and freshly ground black pepper
100 g (3½ oz/scant ½ cup) crème fraîche

Chanterelles fried in butter

rapeseed or peanut oil, for frying
150–200 g (5–7 oz) chanterelles
2–3 garlic cloves
2 tablespoons butter
sea salt and freshly ground black pepper

To serve

6 burger buns, halved
butter for the buns
some dill and thyme

1　Preheat the oven to 180°C (350°F/Gas 4).

2　Scrub the celeriacs clean under running water. Then fully dry them.

3　Heat plenty of oil in a frying pan (skillet) and flash-fry the celeriacs all over until the skin is golden brown (do not cut them up). Transfer them to an ovenproof dish and sprinkle with salt and pepper. Bake for about 2 hours, or until they are soft on the inside.

4　For the herb cream, mix together the herbs, lemon juice and olive oil using a hand blender or food processor. Add salt and pepper to taste. Pour the crème fraîche into a bowl and sprinkle the herb mixture over it, while carefully stirring with a fork so as to create a delicate marbling on the surface. Put to one side.

5　For the chanterelles, heat the oil in a frying pan until it starts to smoke. Toss in the chanterelles and flash-fry them for a minute or so. Peel the garlic cloves, crush them with the thick edge of a knife and put them in the pan together with the butter. Reduce the heat and fry until the mushrooms develop a nice colour.

6　Butter the buns on the cut surface and fry them quickly in a frying pan or grill (broil) them in the oven.

7　Cut the roasted celeriac into 1 cm- (½ in-) thick slices and put 2–3 slices on each bun. Splash on a little herb cream, put a fistful of mushrooms on top and finish off with herbs.

Table barbecues are common in both Japan and Korea. They are designed to provide a good, even heat. They usually get very hot, so keep an eye on what you are grilling. Put ingredients on a skewer or use tongs to ensure you can quickly turn things when necessary. An investment in a table barbecue is an investment in social grilling! They are great for gathering around and are also easy to handle and use.

HARISSA-MARINATED SWEET POTATO
with grilled cabbage leaves and black dukkah

Serves 6

2 medium sweet potatoes

120 g (4 oz) cabbage leaves

1 tablespoon rapeseed (canola) oil

1 pinch of salt

Harissa marinade

4 tablespoons rapeseed (canola) oil

2 tablespoons Harissa (page 207)

1 pinch of ground cumin

juice of 1 lime

1 tablespoon cane sugar

1 garlic clove

To serve

Black Dukkah (page 204)

oregano leaves

sea salt flakes

1 Mix all the marinade ingredients together using a hand-held blender or food processor.

2 Scrub the sweet potatoes under running water and dry thoroughly. Cut the sweet potatoes into slices around 1 cm (½ in) thick and place them on baking parchment. Brush them with the marinade, turn the slices over and brush the other side.

3 Light the charcoal in the table barbecue (grill) and let it take on a fine, soft glow. Grill the sweet potato slices on the barbecue, occasionally turning them over and brushing them with a little more marinade. Once the sweet potatoes start to take on a nice, caramelised golden-brown colour, they are done. Set aside and brush them with more marinade.

4 Place the cabbage leaves in a mixing bowl and massage in the oil and salt. Place the cabbage leaves on the barbecue – they will cook quickly, so have tongs or tweezers close at hand. Turn them a few times so that you can see the leaves taking on colour on both sides.

5 Place a few cabbage leaves on a plate, add a few slices of sweet potato on top and finish off with Black Dukkah, oregano leaves and sea salt flakes.

SRIRACHA-MARINATED BROCCOLI
with shiitake and shiso broth

Serves 6

2 large heads of broccoli, about 300–400 g
(10½–14 oz)

Marinade

3 tablespoons rapeseed (canola) oil

2 tablespoons tamari

1 tablespoon sriracha

1 teaspoon vinegar, 12 per cent

1 teaspoon light miso

1 teaspoon cane sugar

1 garlic clove

1 teaspoon toasted sesame oil

Shiitake mushroom and shiso broth

20 g (¾ oz) dried shiitake

500 ml (17 fl oz/2 cups) water

6 cm (2½ in) leek, white part only

2 tablespoons cold-pressed rapeseed (canola) oil

4–5 shiitake, washed

2 garlic cloves, crushed with the skin on

2 tablespoons sake

1 tablespoon mirin

1 teaspoon freshly grated ginger root

4–5 Sichuan peppercorns

1 cm (½ in) strip unwaxed lime peel

500 ml (17 fl oz/2 cups) Vegetable Stock
(page 196)

2 large shiso leaves

To serve

broccoli florets

2 tablespoons oregano leaves

2 tablespoons small shiso leaves

1 tablespoon finely chopped green chilli

6 teaspoons toasted sesame oil

1 Mix all the marinade ingredients together using a hand-held blender or food processor.

2 Cut the small florets of broccoli off the stalk and set aside. Next, cut the stalk lengthways into four pieces then into four in the opposite direction.

3 Put the pieces of broccoli stalk onto a skewer, brush with marinade and put on a plate.

4 Put the dried mushrooms in a mixing bowl and pour over the boiling water, cover and leave for 20 minutes. Drain the mushrooms (reserving the liquid), dry them on paper towels and set aside. Cut the leeks into thin strips. Pour the oil into a stainless steel saucepan on a medium heat. Add the leeks and fry for around 10 minutes until soft. Add the fresh mushrooms and garlic. Fry while stirring for around 5 minutes. Add the rest of the ingredients for the broth except for the shiso leaves. Mix well. Raise the heat, adding the reserved liquid from the mushrooms and bring to the boil so that it reduces slightly, around 10 minutes. Remove the pan from the heat and add the shiso leaves. Leave to stand, covered with a lid, for a further 20 minutes. Strain the broth into a second saucepan and keep warm.

5 Light the charcoal in the table barbecue (grill) and wait for it to take on a soft glow. Barbecue the broccoli skewers directly on the charcoal, turning them occasionally and brushing them often with more marinade. Once the broccoli starts to caramelise, they are done. Set aside and brush again.

6 Pour around 100 ml (3½ fl oz/scant ½ cup) of broth onto each plate. Add a skewer, top with the reserved small broccoli florets, herbs and chilli. Drizzle sesame oil on top.

APPLE AND BRUSSELS SPROUTS SKEWERS
with whisky-pickled mustard seeds

Serves 6

5 small apples, quartered

18 Brussels sprouts

4 unwaxed lemons

6 tablespoons melted unsalted butter

3 teaspoons cane sugar

To serve

Whisky-pickled Mustard Seeds,

    (page 210)

1   Put three pieces of apple and three Brussels sprouts onto each wooden skewer. Squeeze some juice from one of the lemons onto the apple pieces to stop them turning brown. Place the skewers on a baking sheet and brush with melted butter.

2   Light the charcoal in the table barbecue (grill) and let it take on a fine, soft glow. Barbecue the apple and Brussels sprouts skewers directly on the charcoal, without using a grill, initially turning them often since it will be so hot. Brush them occasionally with more butter. Once the apples begin to take on a nice, caramelised golden-brown colour and the Brussels sprouts are slightly burnt, they are ready. Set aside and brush again with butter.

3   Place on the barbecue. Halve the remaining three lemons and sprinkle sugar on the cut edges. Use your fingers to press the sugar into the flesh of the fruit. Grill the lemons with the cut edge facing down so that they turn golden brown and the sugar caramelises.

4   Place the skewers onto a chopping board and sprinkle the Whisky-pickled Mustard Seeds on top. Serve alongside a half lemon.

HASSELBACK KING OYSTERS

Serves 6

6 large king oysters

6 Smoked Onions (page 208)

Marinade

4 tablespoons rapeseed (canola) oil

1 tablespoon light miso

1 tablespoon tamari

juice of ½ lime

1 teaspoon honey

1 garlic clove

1 teaspoon sesame oil

Soup base

3 tablespoons smoked rapeseed (canola)
   oil from the onion halves above

70 g (2½ oz) finely chopped shallots

100 ml (3½ fl oz/scant ½ cup) sherry

200 ml (7 fl oz/scant 1 cup) Vegetable Stock,
   (page 196)

1 tablespoon light miso

600 ml (20 fl oz/2½ cups) almond milk

To serve

sea salt flakes

1   Mix all the marinade ingredients together using a hand-held blender or food processor.

2   Put the mushrooms on a wooden skewer and make diagonal cuts into them at intervals of 4–5 mm (¼ in). Turn the mushrooms over and do the same on the other side. Brush with the marinade and place on a baking sheet.

3   Pour the smoked rapeseed oil into a cold saucepan, add the shallots and put on a medium heat. Stir constantly using a wooden spoon and cook until the shallots soften but without taking on any colour, around 10 minutes. Pour over the sherry, raise the heat and leave to cook for 5 minutes. Add the Vegetable Stock, miso and almond milk, reduce the heat and whisk thoroughly to ensure everything is mixed. Leave to simmer for a further 10 minutes. Remove from the heat and use a hand-held blender to blend the soup until smooth. Cover with a lid and set aside.

4   Light the charcoal in the table barbecue (grill) and let it take on a fine, soft glow. Barbecue the mushrooms directly on the charcoal, without using a grill, initially turning them often since it is so hot. Brush them occasionally with more marinade. Once the mushrooms take on a nice, caramelised golden-brown colour, they are done. Set aside and brush again with marinade. Add the grill to the table barbecue and grill the Smoked Onions so that they warm up and their skins are slightly burnt. Brush them with their own smoked oil and set aside.

5   Divide the soup between 6 bowls. Break apart the onions and add the pieces to the soup. Add a mushroom to each bowl and top with a few sea salt flakes.

TURNIP SKEWERS with grilled collard greens and sour tomato sauce

Serves 6

12 small turnips, halved

3 tablespoons rapeseed (canola) oil

300 g (10½ oz) collard greens or any
    type of leafy green, e.g. black
    or green kale

1 teaspoon salt

To serve

dill fronds

fennel flowers or fennel dill

mild chilli powder, e.g. piment d'Espelette

sea salt flakes

600 ml (20 fl oz/2½ cups) Fermented
    Yellow Tomato Sauce (page 200)

1   Light the table barbecue (grill) and let the charcoal take on a strong, even glow.

2   Put four turnip halves onto each wooden skewer and brush them with oil. Put them on the grill with the cut edge facing down and grill for 3–4 minutes, or until they begin to take on some colour. Turn them over and grill the other side for about the same amount of time – take care to ensure they don't burn. Wrap the skewers in foil and set aside.

3   Place your chosen greens in a small bowl and drizzle 2 tablespoons of oil over them. Sprinkle with the salt and massage the oil and salt into the leaves. Barbecue them on the grill or in a flour sifter (see tip on page 124) until they turn crisp and take on some colour. Set aside.

4   Set out six bowls and place a fistful of greens in the bottom of each one. Place a skewer on each bowl and top with dill, fennel flowers or fennel dill, the chilli powder and salt. Serve with the Fermented Yellow Tomato Sauce alongside.

SANGRITAS made with grilled chillies and sour beer

Serves 6

12 red chillies (strength according to preference)

1 teaspoon sea salt flakes

½ teaspoon coriander seeds

½ teaspoon black peppercorns

240 ml (8½ fl oz/1 cup) tomato juice

To serve

6 teaspoons mild chilli powder, e.g. piment
   d'Espelette

3 teaspoons salt

1 lime wedge

ice

1.2 litres (40 fl oz/4¾ cups) sour beer,
   preferably a fruity variety based on
   citrus fruits or berries

6 shots of mezcal, 60 ml (2 fl oz/¼ cup) each

1 Light the table barbecue (grill) and grill the chillies while the fire is still burning so that their skins blacken. Place the chillies in a plastic bag with the salt and let them steam in their own heat. Once they have cooled down, after 10–15 minutes, rub the skin off by massaging the chillies while they are still in the bag. Remove the chillies from the bag and split them lengthways. Remove the seeds and set aside.

2 Heat a cast-iron pan on a medium heat. Toast the reserved chilli seeds, coriander seeds and black peppercorns until the seeds turn golden brown and release their aroma. Crush them coarsely using a pestle and mortar.

3 Mix the chillies and spices together with the tomato juice and blend until smooth, using a hand-held blender or food processor. Strain into a mixing bowl.

4 Mix the chilli powder with the salt and put on a plate. Prepare drinking glasses by running the wedge of lime along a quarter of the rim of the glass and then dipping that part into the chilli and salt mix. Add ice to each glass and pour around 50 ml (1¾ fl oz/ 3 tablespoons) of the tomato juice mixture into each one. Add 200 ml (7 fl oz/scant 1 cup) of sour beer and stir genly. Serve alongside a shot of mezcal.

ALEX'S FERMENTED POTATO TORTILLAS

Serves 6

Fermented potatoes

600 g (1 lb 5 oz) large potatoes

9 g (2 teaspoons) salt, without iodine

Potato tortillas

500 g (1 lb 2 oz) fermented potatoes
   (including the liquid that is formed)

25 g (1 oz/¼ cup) organic rye flour

175 g (6 oz/1½ cups) organic plain
   (all-purpose) flour

rapeseed (canola) oil

1 Start with the potatoes. Set the oven to 180°C (350°F/Gas 6). Bake the potatoes for around 1 hour. Remove them from the oven and set aside until they are cool enough to handle. Hollow out the potatoes and place the flesh in a mixing bowl – you should get around 500 g (1 lb 2 oz).

2 Add the salt – it should be 1.8 per cent of the weight of the potatoes in the bowl. Mix without mashing the potatoes too much – there should be some big bits left. Place the mixture into ziplock bags and remove as much air as possible. Leave the bags at room temperature for 3–4 days. They will expand slightly, and liquid will be released. Turn them over occasionally during the process.

3 After 3–4 days at room temperature, the lactic acid bacteria will have eaten up all the available sugar and the potatoes will be fermented. You can either make the dough straight away, or store the potatoes in the refrigerator until you need them. You can also freeze the fermented potatoes to use later on.

4 Pour the fermented potatoes, including all the liquid, into a mixing bowl and add the flour a little at a time. Some types of flour bind with liquid more than others, so use trial and error to find the right amount. Mix the dough with your hands or use a potato masher to begin with to mash the bigger bits of potato then shape the dough into a ball. It will be fairly sticky, but should still hold together well. If it seems dry, add a little water at intervals until it is nice and soft.

5 Split the dough into smaller pieces and roll these into small balls, about 2 cm (¾ in) in diameter. Place them on a plate with plenty of rye flour to stop them from sticking together. Leave to rest for around 10 minutes.

6 Cut out a sheet of baking parchment that is slightly larger than your tortilla press. Take a sheet of baking parchment and position it in the press, drip a little oil in the middle of the parchment and place the ball on top. Take another sheet of parchment, drip a little oil on it and then position it on top of the ball. Press it gently to ensure it stays in place when you close the press. Press the ball into a tortilla about 2 mm (⅛ in) thick.

7 While still between the sheets of paper, place the tortilla in a dry, warm – verging on hot – frying pan (skillet). Fry for 30 seconds, turn over and remove the paper from the fried side. Fry the other side for 30 seconds, turn it over again and remove the second sheet of paper.

8 Remove the tortilla and place it between two dish (tea) towels while you make the rest. I usually run with two frying pans at once. You have to experiment a little on the frying pan temperature until you find a level where the tortillas speckle and puff up a bit without getting burnt.

TACOS WITH BLACK MOLE, SMOKED TOMATOES, CORIANDER ROOT AND COTIJA CHEESE

Serves 6

Black mole

1 large tomato, halved

100 g (3½ oz) sourdough bread

2 tablespoons pecans, crushed

2 tablespoons almonds, crushed

1 tablespoon rapeseed (canola) oil

50 g (2 oz) dried ancho chillies

50 g (2 oz) dried chipotle chillies

2 small yellow onions, quartered

2 garlic cloves, finely chopped

1 teaspoon dried thyme

1 teaspoon dried oregano

2 tablespoons black sesame seeds

1 pinch of ground cinnamon

5 black peppercorns

1 pinch of freshly grated nutmeg

4 cloves

1 teaspoon freshly grated ginger root

130 g (4 oz) raisins

400 ml (13 fl oz/generous 1½ cups) Vegetable
   Stock (page 196)

To serve

6 Fermented Potato Tortillas (page 76)

18 small Smoked Tomatoes (page 208)

coriander (cilantro), picked leaves and finely
   chopped roots (I usually buy whole coriander
   with roots in Asian grocery stores – the roots
   of those grown in pots are too slender)

60 g (2 oz) Cotija, or another hard cheese
   such as pecorino or Parmesan

1 Start with the mole. Light the table barbecue (grill) and let the charcoal take on a fine, soft glow. Grill the tomato halves with the cut edge facing down until the outside has blackened somewhat.

2 Tear the bread into small pieces and place together with the pecans and almonds in a dry cast-iron pan and put on the barbecue. Drip a little oil on top and shake the pan occasionally to ensure everything toasts evenly, around 5–10 minutes. Place the mixture in a mixing bowl and set aside.

3 Slice open the chillies and remove the seeds and set these aside. Place the chillies in a food processor and blend into a powder. Set aside. Put the reserved chilli seeds in the cast-iron pan and toast them until they are burnt and completely black, around 5 minutes. Put the burnt seeds in a bowl and pour 200 ml (7 fl oz/scant 1 cup) of cold water over them. Leave to stand for 1½ hours. Strain and set aside.

4 Return the cast-iron pan to the barbecue to a spot where the temperature is lower. Pour in the remaining oil, add the onions and tomato and leave to cook for 15 minutes, stirring occasionally. Add the garlic and cook for a further 10 minutes.

5 Then add the thyme, oregano, sesame seeds, cinnamon, peppercorns, nutmeg, cloves, ginger and raisins. Stir for 2–3 minutes to ensure that everything is well mixed. Add the bread and nut mix, chilli powder, chilli seeds and Vegetable Stock and cook for around 10 minutes.

6 Pour the mole into a food processor and blend until smooth. Pour everything back into the cast-iron pan and leave to cook for a further 30 minutes. Stir occasionally to ensure it does not burn. Add a little water if it gets too dry.

7 Place a Tortilla onto each plate and dollop 2 tablespoons of the mole onto each one. Top with three Smoked Tomatoes, coriander and finish by grating the cheese over it.

TACOS WITH GRILLED AVOCADO, PICKLED RED ONIONS AND CHILLI SAUCE

Serves 6

3–4 medium avocados

juice of 1 lime

rapeseed (canola) oil

To serve

6 Fermented Potato Tortillas (page 76)

Pickled Red Onions (page 196)

hot chilli sauce, e.g. Midsummer's Louisiana Hot
    Sauce (page 207)

1   Light the table barbecue (grill) and let the charcoal take on a strong, even glow. Halve the avocados and remove the stones. Carefully hollow them out using a spoon and then cut the biggest possible slices lengthways, around 1 cm (⅓ in) thick. Place the slices on a plate and brush them with lime juice and then oil.

2   Grill the avocado slices quickly on a really high heat. The outsides should be caramelised and almost burnt, while inside the avocados should be cold and retain their consistency.

3   Place a Tortilla on each plate and top with a few slices of avocado. Finish with Pickled Red Onions and drizzle a little chilli sauce on top according to your preference.

TACOS WITH KING OYSTERS AND PINEAPPLE

Serves 6

3 large king oysters, torn into long pieces

1 tablespoon rapeseed (canola) oil

6 pieces of Roasted Pineapple, see recipe
    (page 104, steps 1 and 3)

Mushroom spice

1½ teaspoons salt

2 teaspoons mild chilli powder, e.g. piment
    d'Espelette

1 teaspoon onion powder

1 teaspoon garlic powder

1 teaspoon smoked paprika

1 pinch of ground cumin

1 pinch of ground cayenne pepper

To serve

6 Fermented Potato Tortillas (page 76)

6 lime wedges

1   Light the table barbecue (grill) and let the charcoal take on a strong, even glow. Mix all the mushroom spice ingredients in a bowl.

2   Place the mushrooms in a bowl with the oil and mix until all the pieces are covered. Sprinkle most of the mushroom spice over and fold into the mushrooms carefully. Place the mushrooms in a double strainer (see tip on page 86) and put on the grill or hold it over the glow. Occasionally shake the strainer, and drip a little oil on at intervals. Open after a few minutes and check whether the mushrooms have taken on any colour, cooking until golden brown. Set aside.

3   Place a Tortilla on each plate, top with pineapple on one side and the mushrooms on the other, season with mushroom spice and serve with a lime wedge.

FENNEL ROOT WITH SHIITAKE, SPRING ONIONS, BUCKWHEAT AND HERB OIL

Serves 6

300 g (10½ oz) fennel roots

1 litre (34 fl oz/4 cups) water

1 teaspoon sea salt flakes

juice of ½ lemon

300 g (10½ oz) shiitake

4 tablespoons rapeseed (canola) oil

Herb oil

4 tablespoons parsley leaves

4 tablespoons mint leaves + 2 tablespoons
   for serving

2–3 tarragon leaves

1 garlic clove

juice of ½ lemon

3 tablespoons olive oil

sea salt flakes and black pepper

Boiled buckwheat

700 ml (24 fl oz/scant 3 cups) water

150 g (5 oz/scant 1 cup) whole buckwheat

2 teaspoons herbal salt

1 sprig of parsley

Grilled and steamed spring onions

3 tablespoons olive oil

6 spring onions (scallions)

sea salt flakes and black pepper

1 Scrub and scrape the fennel roots clean. Place them in a bowl with the water, salt and lemon juice. Cover with cling film (plastic wrap) and leave in the refrigerator overnight.

2 Make the herb oil by blending the herbs, garlic, lemon juice and olive oil using a hand-held blender or food processor. Season with salt and pepper to taste.

3 Boil the water for the buckwheat in a saucepan. Rinse the buckwheat in a sieve (fine-mesh strainer), first in hot water and then cold. Reduce to a low heat, then add the buckwheat, salt and parsley. Cook for 10 minutes, stirring occasionally. Remove from the heat and leave to stand and swell for 15 minutes.

4 Light the table barbecue (grill). Pour olive oil into a plastic bag big enough to fit the spring onions and keep near to the barbecue. Season the spring onions with salt and pepper and put them on the barbecue while the charcoal is still burning. Grill the spring onions so that the surface is slightly burnt. Remove the spring onions using tongs and place in the plastic bag. Knot the bag and shake it so that the oil covers all of the spring onions. Leave the spring onions in the bag for around 20 minutes so that they are steamed in their own heat.

5 Clean the shiitake mushrooms and cut up larger mushrooms so that all pieces are about the same size. Place them in a bowl with 1½ tablespoons of rapeseed oil and a little salt and pepper, and mix to ensure they are properly covered. Place the mushrooms in a double strainer (see tip on page 86) and put this on the barbecue or hold it over the glow. Occasionally shake the strainer, and drip a little oil on at intervals. Open after a few minutes and check whether the mushrooms have taken on any colour. They will be done when they turn a lovely golden brown. Set aside.

6 Remove the fennel roots from the water and dry them. Repeat the same procedure as with the mushrooms in step 5.

7 Spoon some buckwheat onto each plate, followed by a few fennel roots, some shiitake mushrooms and a spring onion split lengthways. Top with herb oil and mint.

GRILLED PIMIENTOS DE PADRÓN
with crème fraîche and grated kombu

Serves 6

300 g (10½ oz) pimientos de Padrón

2 tablespoons rapeseed (canola) oil

sea salt flakes

300 ml (10 fl oz/1¼ cups) crème fraîche

2 teaspoons mild chilli powder, e.g. piment
    d'Espelette

1 teaspoon sesame seeds (preferably a mixture
    of colours)

kombu leaves (available from Asian grocery stores)

1 Light the table barbecue (grill) and let the charcoal take on a fine, even glow.

2 Place the chillies in a bowl, cover with oil and massage until everything is covered. Place the chillies in a coarse mesh strainer and grill until they take on colour and their skin starts to bubble and crack. Remove from the grill and season with sea salt flakes to taste.

3 Dollop crème fraîche onto a plate, sprinkle chilli powder and sesame seeds on top and grate the kombu over it using a zester. Place the chillies on top and serve immediately.

USE A DOUBLE STRAINER FOR SMALL INGREDIENTS **To ensure that smaller ingredients such as Padrón chillies and mushrooms don't fall through the grill, use a double strainer. Take two equal sized, coarse mesh strainers, put what you want to grill inside and wrap the two handles together tightly using steel wire.**

02

INDIRECT HEAT

FRENCH STRING BEANS with charcoal-roasted shallots and crème fraîche with garlic and herbs

Serves 6

18 shallots, with the skin on

600 g (1 lb 5 oz) French string beans

2 tablespoons rapeseed (canola) oil

Herb oil

10 g (½ oz) mixed chopped herbs,
    e.g. oregano, thyme and dill

2 garlic cloves

juice of ½ lemon

3 tablespoons olive oil

sea salt flakes and black pepper

To serve

200 ml (7 fl oz/scant 1 cup) crème fraîche

sea salt flakes

1 Start with the herb oil. Blend the herbs, garlic, lemon juice and olive oil using a hand-held blender or food processor. Season with salt and pepper to taste.

2 Add charcoal or firewood to half of the barbecue (grill) so that you have space to roast the onions using indirect heat later. Light the barbecue and once it is burning strongly, place the shallots straight onto the charcoal so that the outer layer burns. Pick up the shallots, place on the grill and position them on the charcoal-free side. Close the lid and roast them using indirect heat for 20–30 minutes until the shallots are soft all the way through. You can measure the core temperature – it will preferably be above 60°C (140°F). Set aside and leave to cool.

3 Trim and wash the beans. Dry them and place in a bowl with the rapeseed oil. Mix well so that everything is covered in the oil. Place the beans on the barbecue straight over the glow and roll them back and forth constantly for around 5 minutes, taking care to ensure they don't burn too much. Remove them from the grill.

4 Pour crème fraîche into a bowl and drizzle two thirds of the herb oil over it at the same time as stirring it gently using a fork to ensure lovely marbling on the surface.

5 Press the shallots out of their burnt skins and cut them in half. Place them together with the beans on a plate. Drizzle the rest of the herb oil over and top with some sea salt flakes. Serve alongside the crème fraîche .

CHARCOAL-ROASTED POINTED CABBAGE
with browned butter and Béarnaise sauce

Serves 6

2 medium pointed cabbage heads (preferably red
as they look best)

Béarnaise sauce

about 30 ml (1 fl oz/⅛ cup) water

3 tablespoons white wine vinegar

1 small shallot, coarsely chopped with the skin on

1 sprig of tarragon

2 white peppercorns

2 Sichuan peppercorns

4 coriander seeds

300 g (10½ oz) unsalted butter

2 egg yolks, at room temperature

To serve

150 g (5 oz) unsalted butter

6 small sprigs of tarragon

1 Add charcoal or firewood to half of the barbecue (grill) so that you have space to roast the cabbage using indirect heat later. Light your barbecue and, once it is burning strongly, place the cabbage straight onto the charcoal so that the outer layer burns. Turn several times using tongs then remove from the charcoal. Place the grill on top and position the cabbage on its side away from the flames. Close the lid and roast using indirect heat for 1 hour until the cabbage feels soft when you gently press the skin. You can measure the core temperature – it should preferably be above 75°C (170°F).

2 Add the water, 2 tablespoons of vinegar, shallots, tarragon and spices to a saucepan. Bring to the boil and reduce to half the volume. Strain the mixture and set aside for now. Prepare a water bath. Boil the water in a saucepan, then remove from the heat and cover with a stainless steel mixing bowl. Melt the butter in a saucepan so that it reaches a temperature of around 50°C (120°F). Pour the egg yolks into the mixing bowl, add the vinegar reduction and start to whisk. Add the butter in a thin and steady stream while whisking continuously. Once you get a good, thick consistency you can stir in a tablespoon of the remaining vinegar towards the end to add a little more acidity to the sauce.

3 Brown the butter for serving. Put a saucepan on a medium heat. Add the butter and start to whisk just as it melts. Continue to whisk until the butter is lovely and golden brown in colour and smells nutty. Remove from the heat and continue to whisk for a little bit to avoid it burning on the bottom.

4 After the cabbage has cooled slightly, peel away the outermost burnt layers. Cut the cabbage into portions and plate up. Spoon over the brown butter, dollop a little Béarnaise sauce over the top and garnish with sprigs of tarragon.

LEEK four ways

Pickled leek

100 ml (3½ fl oz/scant ½ cup) vinegar,
    12 per cent

180 g (6 oz/scant 1 cup) caster (superfine) sugar

300 ml (10 fl oz/1¼ cups) water for the
    syrup + 500 ml (17 fl oz/2 cups) for blanching

1 leek

100 g (3½ oz/⅓ cup) salt

Leek ash

leftover parts from the pickled leek

Grilled leek

2 large leeks

Leek and parsley mayonnaise

100 ml (3½ fl oz/scant ½ cup) olive oil

leftover parts of the leek from the grilled leek

10 g (½ oz) parsley leaves

400 ml (13 fl oz/generous 1½ cups) Mayonnaise
    using Eggs (page 202)

To serve

6 teaspoons toasted sesame oil

6 tablespoons finely chopped cashews

sea salt flakes

1 Start with the pickled leek – it needs 24 hours in the refrigerator. Boil the vinegar, sugar and 300 ml (10 fl oz/1¼ cups) of water in a saucepan. Wash and remove the outer layer of the leek, save the green parts for making the leek ash. Cut the leek into slices ½ cm (¼ in) thick and press out the leek rings as much as possible. Boil 500 ml (17 fl oz/2 cups) of water in a saucepan with the salt. Blanch the leek rings in the hot water for a few seconds then drain in a colander and rinse the leeks under cold running water. Place the leeks in a bowl and pour the syrup over, cover with a lid or cling film (plastic wrap) and put in the refrigerator.

2 To make the leek ash, set the oven to the highest temperature. Take the leftover green parts from the leeks and cut into long, thin, flat pieces. Place them on a baking sheet and put in the oven for a few minutes until the leeks are completely black. Remove the baking sheet and turn over the leaves. Return to the oven and let the other side turn black. Remove and leave to cool. Use a hand-held blender or food processor to blend the black leaves into a fine powder.

3 Add charcoal or firewood to half of the barbecue (grill) so that you have space to roast the leeks using indirect heat later. Light the barbecue and once it is burning strongly, place the leeks on the grill or straight onto the charcoal so that the outer layer burns. Put the grill on top of the barbecue and position the leeks on the side away from the flames. Close the lid and roast using indirect heat for 20–30 minutes until the leeks are soft all the way through. You can measure the core temperature – it should preferably be above 85°C (185°F) in the middle.

4 Cut the leek into pieces as shown in the picture on page 95, then set the diagonally cut pieces aside. Use the leftover pieces for the mayonnaise.

5 Warm up the olive oil in a saucepan over a medium heat, then add the leftover pieces of leek together with the parsley. Cook until soft, around 10 minutes. Pour everything into a food processor. Blend until smooth then pour the mixture into a mixing bowl and leave to cool. Add the mayonnaise and stir to ensure everything is well combined.

6 Place a piece of grilled leek onto each plate. Drizzle a teaspoon of sesame oil, add some cashew crumbs along the sides and top with the pickled leeks. Sprinkle a few pinches of leek ash and dollop a generous spoonful of mayonnaise on top.

ROASTED CELERIAC with grilled chicory, chanterelles, chicory dukkah and herb cream

Serves 6

chicory (endive) leaves; alternatively dandelion,
    radicchio or other bitter leaves
sea salt flakes
2 tablespoons white wine vinegar
3 small celeriac (celery roots)

Herb cream

10 g (½ oz) fresh mixed herbs, e.g. thyme,
    rosemary and dill
juice of ½ lemon
3 tablespoons olive oil
salt and black pepper
100 ml (3½ fl oz/scant ½ cup) crème fraîche

Grilled chanterelles

150–200 g (5–7 oz) chanterelles
2–3 garlic cloves, lightly crushed
1 tablespoon rapeseed (canola) or peanut oil
salt and black pepper

To serve

Chicory Dukkah or ordinary Dukkah,
    (page 204)
chicory (endive) flowers
sea salt flakes

1 Soak the chicory leaves in the vinegar, mixed with a good pinch of salt. Leave to stand until serving.

2 Add charcoal or firewood to half of the barbecue (grill) so that you have space to roast the celeriac using indirect heat later. Light the barbecue and once it is burning strongly, place the celeriac onto the grill so that the outer layer burns. Place the celeriac on the side away from the flames, close the lid and using indirect heat roast for 1½ hours until the celeriac feels soft when you press the skin. You can measure the core temperature, which should ideally be above 60°C (140°F).

3 Make the herb cream. Using a hand-held blender or food processor, blend the herbs, lemon juice and olive oil. Season with salt and pepper to taste. Pour the herb mix into a mixing bowl, add the crème fraîche and mix thoroughly.

4 Trim and brush away any dirt from the chanterelles. Place them in a bowl together with the garlic. Add the oil, season with salt and pepper and turn over. Then place the chanterelles in a double strainer (see tip on page 86) and put this on the grill or hold it over the glow. Occasionally shake the strainer, and pour a little oil on at intervals. Open after a few minutes and check whether the mushrooms have taken on any colour. They will be done when they turn a lovely golden brown. Set aside for now.

5 Remove the chicory leaves from the water and dry them either using paper towels or with a salad spinner.

6 Peel the celeriac once they have cooled slightly. You can usually do this with your fingers, but you can otherwise cut the skin off using a knife. Try to keep as much as possible of the roasted vegetable just inside the skin intact. Cut each celeriac into four pieces.

7 Dollop a generous spoonful of herb cream onto each plate, sprinkle 2 tablespoons of Dukkah and add two pieces of celeriac to each. Top with chicory leaves and mushrooms. Garnish with the flowers or a suitable herb.

I often choose to roast larger, more compact vegetables or fruits until the skin is burnt and completely black, before cooking them using indirect heat for a little longer. This is an amazing way of producing the wonderful charred barbecue flavour while also cooking the insides without them drying out and getting boring, which can happen if you slice them and barbecue them.

ROASTED PINEAPPLE with rum
coconut cream

Serves 6

3 medium pineapples

Rum coconut cream

1 vanilla pod (bean)

200 ml (7 fl oz/scant 1 cup) coconut cream

100 ml (3½ fl oz/scant ½ cup) crème fraîche

2 tablespoons dark rum

1 tablespoon cane sugar

To serve

1 unwaxed lime, finely zested

lemon verbena

1 Light the barbecue (grill). Pierce a few holes into each pineapple using a skewer and place them straight onto the glowing charcoal – you can even do this while it is still burning. Roast the pineapple until the skin is completely charred and soft inside – this will take 1–2 hours or longer. The skin is very thick, so it can withstand being left for a while. You can tell it is almost done when the pineapple has shrunk slightly and the skin is slightly soft when you press it. You can measure the core temperature – it should preferably be above 80–90°C (175–195°F).

2 Make the cream while the pineapple is in the charcoal. Cut the vanilla pod lengthways and scrape the seeds into a bowl. Add the remaining ingredients and whip the cream as firmly as possible. I usually put it in the freezer for an hour before eating it so that it is extra firm when served.

3 Cut the top off the pineapple and then set it upright. Cut off the outermost black skin, but try to keep as much of the brown flesh close to the skin as possible without too much of the charred layer remaining, then cut into quarters lengthways. I usually remove the core from the middle, which is often slightly too tough after being roasted for a long time.

4 Place two pieces of pineapple on each plate, dollop a generous spoonful of coconut cream onto them and top with finely grated lime zest and lemon verbena.

SMOKY PINEAPPLE SOUR

Serves 6

300 g (10½ oz) Roasted Pineapple, see
     steps 1 and 3 in the recipe to the left
120 ml (4 fl oz/½ cup) agave syrup
1 teaspoon chopped green chilli
3 cm (1½ in) fresh ginger root, peeled
120 ml (4 fl oz/½ cup) lime juice
600 ml (20 fl oz/2½ cups) pineapple juice
1 cinnamon stick, around 4 cm (1¾ in)
300 ml (10 fl oz/1¼ cups) gin
3 egg whites

To serve

smoke wood chips
ice
cinnamon stick
6 dried pineapple slices

1   Place the charcoal-roasted pineapple, syrup, chilli, ginger, lime and pineapple juice into a food processor and pulse several times. Pour into a mixing bowl, add the cinnamon stick and leave in the refrigerator overnight.

2   Put the glasses in the refrigerator around an hour before serving the drinks. Strain the pineapple mixture into a jug. Press hard to ensure you get a little of the pineapple flesh in the mixture.

3   Use a cocktail shaker big enough for two drinks. Add around 400 ml (13 fl oz/generous 1½ cups) of the pineapple mixture, 100 ml (3½ fl oz/scant ½ cup) of gin and 1 egg white.

4   Shake once without ice to add air to the drink and let the egg white fluff up. Fill the shaker with ice and shake again until the metal feels cold.

5   Ignite some of the smoke wood chips and place on a baking sheet. Turn the glasses upside down and place over the chips so that smoke collects inside them. The cold glass will cool the smoke so that it stays in place when you turn them back over.

6   Turn the glasses over carefully so that you don't lose too much smoke. Add ice and slowly pour half of the liquid from the shaker, top with a little grated cinnamon and a slice of dried pineapple.

ROASTED AND SMOKED POTATOES
with beer-caramelised onions

Serves 6

6 medium potatoes (small baking potatoes)

100–200 g (3½–7 oz) applewood smoker chips

Caramelised onion mixture

6 medium yellow onions, chopped

3 tablespoons unsalted butter

200 ml (7 fl oz/scant 1 cup) beer, preferably lager

To serve

Pickled Wild Garlic Capers (page 211)

oregano leaves

watercress

sea salt flakes

1 Add charcoal or firewood to half of the barbecue (grill) so that you have space to roast the potatoes using indirect heat later. Light the barbecue and add a fistful of smoker chips to the glow once the flames have begun to die down. Place the potatoes on the grill on the side where there are no flames, cover with the lid and roast them using indirect heat for around 1 hour, turning them occasionally. The potatoes will be done when they feel soft when you gently touch the skin. You can measure the core temperature – it should preferably be above 90°C (195°F).

2 Place the onions and butter in a cold terrine dish or saucepan. Warm up on the grill on a medium heat and cover with a lid. The onions will soon start to release liquid and the flavours will be concentrated through the onions cooking in their own juices. Stir using a wooden spoon about every 5 minutes for 30–40 minutes. Take care to make sure it does not burn (if you notice it getting too dry, you can add the beer earlier.) Add the beer, raise the heat and reduce the mixture substantially. Stir frequently, preferably towards the end when almost all the liquid has been reduced down – this should take around 20 minutes. Set the terrine to one side.

3 Cut an incision into each potato and squeeze the ends so that it opens up. Add a generous dollop of onions to each cut and top with Pickled Wild Garlic Capers, oregano, watercress and salt.

ROASTED SWEDE with grilled shiitake and lovage broth

Serves 6

3 medium swedes
300 g (10½ oz) shiitake

Lovage broth

1 litre (34 fl oz/4 cups) water
20 g (¾ oz) dried shiitake
2 tablespoons cold-pressed rapeseed (canola) oil
300 g (10½ oz) pearl onions, peeled
2 garlic cloves, crushed with the skin on
1 tablespoon white wine vinegar
2 bay leaves
1 white peppercorn
1 cm (½ in) strip of unwaxed lemon peel
2–3 sprigs of lovage

To serve

lovage leaves
1 tablespoon cold-pressed rapeseed (canola) oil
sea salt flakes and pepper

1   Add charcoal or firewood to half of the barbecue (grill) so that you have space to roast the swede using indirect heat later. Light the barbecue and once it is burning strongly, place the swede straight onto the charcoal so that the outer layers burn. Turn several times using tongs. Place the grill on top and position the swede on the side away from the flames. Close the lid and roast using indirect heat for 1 hour until the swede feels soft when you gently press the skin. You can measure the core temperature – it should preferably be above 85°C (185°F) in the middle. Set aside to cool.

2   Boil water for the broth. Place the dried mushrooms in a mixing bowl, cover with boiling water, place a lid on top and leave to stand for 20 minutes. Strain the mushrooms and reserve the liquid. Dry the mushrooms using paper towels and set aside. Pour the oil into a stainless steel saucepan and put on a medium heat. Add the onions and fry until soft but without taking on any colour, around 10 minutes. Add the rehydrated mushrooms and garlic and stir for around 5 minutes. Add the vinegar, bay leaves, peppercorn and lemon peel. Stir to make sure that everything is well combined. Turn up the heat, add the reserved mushroom broth and bring to the boil so that it reduces slightly, around 10 minutes. Remove the pan from the heat, add the lovage and leave to stand covered with a lid for a further 20 minutes. Remove the pearl onions and set aside. Strain the rest of the broth into a second saucepan and keep it warm.

3   Trim and brush clean the fresh shiitake mushrooms. Grill them using a double strainer (see tip on page 86) or fry them hard in a cast-iron pan with a little oil.

4   Peel the swede once it has cooled slightly. Do this with your fingers, or cut the skin off using a knife. Try to keep as much as possible of the roasted vegetables. Then cut it into slices around 3–4 mm (⅛ in) thick.

5   Place a few slices of swede into a soup bowl, quarter the onions and place a few beside the swede. Pour over the broth, add a few shiitake mushrooms and lovage leaves. Drizzle over a little cold-pressed rapeseed oil and season with salt and pepper.

ROASTED SWEDE ON A BED OF SHISO
with sour cream, horseradish and chervil

Serves 6

1 small swede

12 shiso or mint leaves

3 tablespoons sour cream

6 teaspoons freshly grated horseradish

6 chervil leaves

sea salt flakes

1 Add charcoal or firewood to half of the barbecue (grill) so that you have space to roast the swede using indirect heat later. Light the barbecue and once it is burning strongly, place the swede straight onto the charcoal so that the outer layer burns. Turn several times using tongs. Place the grill on top and position the swede on its side away from the flames. Close the lid and roast using indirect heat for 1 hour until the swede feels soft when you gently press the skin. You can measure the core temperature – it should preferably be above 85°C (185°F).

2 Peel the swede once it has cooled slightly. You can usually do this with your fingers, but you can otherwise cut the skin off using a knife. Try to keep as much as possible of the roasted vegetable just inside its skin.

3 Cut the swede into four and then cut into slices 3–4 mm (⅛ in) thick. Place the shiso leaves on plates and position a couple of slices of swede on top of each one. Dollop ½ tablespoon of sour cream onto each one, followed by 1 teaspoon of horseradish. Top with chervil leaves and a scattering of sea salt.

MAKE A DOUBLE BATCH **This is supposed to be a snack to go with your aperitif, but naturally you can double the recipe. They are usually popular, so don't be mean – make more!**

LOVE'S charcoal-roasted celeriac drink

Serves 6

2 medium celeriac (celery roots)

3 tablespoons unsalted butter

240 ml (8½ fl oz/1 cup) lemon juice

100 ml (3½ fl oz/scant ½ cup) sugar syrup

    (1 part caster/superfine) sugar + 1 part water)

360 ml (12 fl oz/1½ cups) mezcal

ice

To serve

large ice cubes

1 Add charcoal or firewood to half of the barbecue (grill) so that you have space to roast the celeriac using indirect heat. Light the barbecue. Once it is burning strongly, place the celeriac straight onto the charcoal so that the outer layer burns. Turn several times using tongs. Place the grill on top and position the celeriac on the grill on the charcoal-free side. Close the lid and roast using indirect heat for 1 hour until the celeriac feels soft when you gently press the skin. You can measure the core temperature – it should be above 90°C (195°F).

2 Leave the celeriac to cool until you can handle them without burning yourself. Cut into four parts and then cut away the white flesh. If you can manage to get a little of the brown flesh just inside the black skin then that is great – there's lots of smoky flavour there.

3 Add the celeriac and butter to a food processor and blend until smooth.

4 Get out a cocktail shaker. For each drink, add 100 ml (3½ fl oz) of celeriac purée, 40 ml (3 tablespoons) of lemon juice, 15 ml (1 tablespoon) of sugar syrup and 60 ml (2 fl oz/¼ cup) of mezcal. Fill with ice cubes, attach the lid and shake away. Check whether it needs more acidity or sweetness, then adjust accordingly by either adding more lemon juice or sugar syrup.

5 Strain the drink into glasses filled with ice.

THE GREEN BARBECUE COOKBOOK

03

STRAIGHT INTO THE FIRE

SALT-ROASTED RED BEETROOT
IN ONION SKINS

Serves 6

Grilled red onions

3 large red onions, halved with skin on

1 tablespoon rapeseed (canola) oil

1 tablespoon red wine vinegar, preferably
    merlot vinegar

1 pinch of dried oregano

1 teaspoon sea salt flakes

Salt-roasted beetroot

4 medium red beetroot

coarse sea salt

6–7 garlic cloves

thyme leaves

2 teaspoons olive oil

10 g (½ oz) finely chopped lemon balm

½ unwaxed lime, finely zested

Cep broth

1 litre (34 fl oz/4 cups) water

20 g (¾ oz) dried ceps

2 tablespoons cold-pressed rapeseed (canola) oil

2 yellow onions, peeled and quartered

2 garlic cloves, crushed with the skin on

1 tablespoon red wine vinegar, preferably
    merlot vinegar

2 bay leaves

1 black peppercorn

1 cm (½ in) strip unwaxed lime peel

2–3 sprigs of parsley

To serve

croutons

Whisky-pickled Mustard Seeds (page 210)

lemon balm

1   Brush the onions with oil on the cut edge. Light the barbecue (grill) and place the onions, cut-side down, on the grill while there are still flames. Hold down using tongs until completely black. Place them in a plastic bag and add the vinegar, oregano and salt. Knot the bag tightly and leave the onions to steam.

2   Cover the bottom of a greased terrine or cast-iron pan with a layer of salt and position the beetroot with a little distance between them. Sprinkle with salt so they are almost covered. Insert the garlic and thyme between the beetroot. Position the terrine directly in the glowing charcoal and roast the beetroots until soft, around 40–50 minutes. When they look slightly shrunken and grey on the outside, they are usually perfectly cooked.

3   Boil the water for the broth. Put the dried ceps in a mixing bowl, cover in the boiling water, cover with a lid and leave to stand for 20 minutes. Strain the ceps and reserve the liquid. Dry the ceps using paper towels and set aside. Pour the rapeseed oil into a saucepan and put on a high heat. Add the onions and fry them hard for around 10 minutes until they take on colour. Add the ceps and garlic and fry while stirring for about 5 minutes. Mix in the vinegar, bay leaves, peppercorn and lime peel. Stir a few times to ensure everything is fully combined. Raise the heat, add the reserved cep broth and bring to the boil so that it reduces slightly, for around 10 minutes. Remove the pan from the heat, add the parsley, and leave to stand covered with a lid for a further 20 minutes. Strain and set aside.

4   Peel the beetroot once they have cooled down slightly and cut them into cubes around 5 x 5 mm (¼ x ¼ in). Place in a bowl with olive oil, lemon balm and finely grated lime zest and mix well.

5   Remove the onions from the bag and rub off the salt and oregano. Remove the larger outer layers of onion so that you have 'onion boats' to put the beetroot in – I usually get 3–4 from each onion half. Plate the 'onion boats', fill with the beetroot mixture and spoon a little broth over them so that the boats fill up. Top with croutons, the Whisky-pickled Mustard Seeds and a little lemon balm.

TARTE TATIN with sweet rye bread and walnuts

Serves 6

Pastry

220 g (8 oz/scant 2 cups) plain (all-purpose) flour

2 teaspoons baking powder

½ teaspoon salt

150 g (5 oz/¾ cup) cane sugar

200 g (7 oz/1 cup) unsalted butter, chilled and cubed

2 eggs

Topping

6 medium apples, peeled and cored

juice of ½ lemon

150 g (5 oz) sweetened rye bread

100 g (3½ oz) walnuts

150 g (5 oz/¾ cup) cane sugar

70 g (2½ oz/⅓ cup) unsalted butter

To serve

vanilla custard

1 Sift the flour and baking powder into a mixing bowl, then add the salt and sugar. Add the cold, cubed butter and rub it into the flour until it has a somewhat sandy consistency. Add the eggs and mix until the dough is lovely and soft. Cover in cling film (plastic wrap) and leave in the refrigerator for at least 30 minutes.

2 Cut the apples into thick wedges and place them in a mixing bowl with some lemon juice to stop them from going brown while you complete the other steps.

3 Put the bread and walnuts into a food processor and pulse so that they are well blended and finely chopped.

4 Light the barbecue (grill) and let the charcoal take on a strong, even glow. Put a cast-iron saucepan on the grill, add the sugar and butter and melt together. Add the apple wedges and leave to simmer on a medium heat for around 15 minutes. Stir occasionally to ensure the apples do not stick.

5 Remove the pan from the heat and distribute the bread and walnut mixture over the apples.

6 Roll the dough out into a circle and place it on top of the apples as a loose lid. The edges should be a fair size and hang down the edge of the pan.

7 Place the pan back on the grill above indirect heat. Press the dough gently down onto the apples. Place the lid on the barbecue and bake for around 1 hour. Aim for a temperature of 150–170°C (300–340°F). Remove the pan and set aside.

8 Let the pie rest for a while until it has settled, then turn it out onto a serving plate. It's best when served with vanilla custard.

There are lots of types of charcoal with different characteristics, but generally the harder the charcoal the better the quality and the more evenly it burns. Japanese binchō-tan is the charcoal of choice of many barbecue geeks. It can maintain an excellent, even heat for many hours and is especially suitable for table barbecues (grills).

SALT-ROASTED PEARS with burrata and grilled black kale

Serves 6

coarse sea salt

6 medium pears

6–7 garlic cloves

thyme and oregano leaves

2–3 black kale leaves per serving

olive oil

3 burrata

sea salt flakes

To serve

olive oil

1–2 unwaxed lemons, finely zested

chive flowers or snipped chives

1 Light the barbecue (grill) and let the charcoal take on a strong, even glow.

2 Layer the bottom of a moist terrine dish or cast-iron pan with sea salt flakes and place the pears on the bed of salt at regular intervals from each other. Sprinkle with sea salt flakes so they are almost covered and insert the garlic and herbs between the pears.

3 Position the terrine directly on the glowing charcoal and roast the pears until soft, around 40–50 minutes. When the pears are slightly shrunken and golden brown on the outside they are usually perfect on the inside.

4 Put the black kale leaves in a small bowl and drizzle with some oil. Sprinkle a little salt over them and massage into the leaves. Barbecue the leaves on the grill or in a flour sifter (as pictured) until they turn crisp and take on some colour. Set aside.

5 Remove the pears from the salt bed and rub off the salt thoroughly. Cut them in half lengthways or quarter them, depending on size. Place a few pieces of pear on each plate and wrap in black kale. Halve the burrata and place a piece on top of each plate. Drizzle with a little olive oil, and top with finely zested lemon rind and a chive flower. If the flowers are out of season, snip some chives over the plate instead.

GRILLING DELICATE INGREDIENTS **When grilling vegetables or herbs and thin cabbage leaves that often fall between the grill or suffer too much in the heat, a flour sifter is a great option. Place it straight on the grill to add a little more distance between the ingredient and the heat, and using tongs to turn delicate ingredients.**

04

VEGETABLES ON CHARCOAL

CHARCOAL-ROASTED CARROTS
with lovage broth

Serves 6

6 medium carrots, preferably purple

Lovage broth

2 litres (70 fl oz/8 cups) Vegetable Stock,
   (page 196)

1 piece of turmeric, about 3 cm (1¼ in), sliced with
   skin on

1 teaspoon black peppercorns

1 teaspoon coriander seeds

1 teaspoon Sichuan pepper

1 tablespoon white wine vinegar, preferably
   Champagne vinegar

1 sprig of lovage

sea salt flakes

To serve

lovage (not too much as it has a very strong,
   potent flavour)

parsley leaves

watercress

cold-pressed rapeseed (canola) oil

1 Start with the broth. Boil the Vegetable Stock together with the turmeric, peppercorns, coriander seeds and Sichuan pepper. Leave to cook for a few minutes then take off the heat. Add the vinegar and lovage. Stir a few times, cover with the lid and leave to stand for around 20 minutes. Strain and season with a little salt.

2 Add charcoal or firewood to half the barbecue (grill) so that you have space to roast the carrots using indirect heat later. Light the barbecue and once it is burning strongly, place the carrots straight onto the charcoal so that the outer layer burns. Turn several times using tongs. Pick up the carrots, place on the grill and position them on the charcoal-free side. Close the lid and roast using indirect heat for around 30 minutes. Remove using tongs and leave to cool.

3 Rub the skin off the carrots, either by using rubber gloves or with a plastic bag. Cut the carrots into slices around 1 cm (½ in) thick.

4 Plate up the carrot slices, top with the herbs and watercress, then finish with broth and a few drops of a flowery, cold-pressed rapeseed oil.

CHARCOAL-ROASTED AUBERGINE with smoked tomatoes, grilled lemon and toasted pine nuts

Serves 6

6 medium aubergines (eggplants)

3 unwaxed lemons

400 ml (13 fl oz/generous 1½ cups) water

1 teaspoon salt

2–3 garlic cloves, crushed

1 sprig of parsley

1 sprig of lovage

1 teaspoon black peppercorns

1 teaspoon coriander seeds

12 Smoked Tomatoes + 2 tablespoons oil
    from the tomato smoking process,
    (page 208)

60 g (2 oz) pine nuts

To serve

1 sprig of parsley

1 Light the barbecue (grill). Pierce the aubergines in a few places using a cocktail stick (toothpick) then place them straight onto the glowing charcoal. This can even be done while the charcoal is still burning. Roast the aubergines until the skin has charred completely and the aubergine is soft inside, around 15 minutes. Place in a mixing bowl and cover with a lid or cling film (plastic wrap) so that they continue to steam and release some liquid.

2 Halve the lemons and grill them on the cut-side down, until they have taken on some colour.

3 Peel the aubergines once they have cooled down enough to be handled without burning yourself. Try to retain as much of the brown flesh just beneath the skin as possible – this is where most of the flavour is – but ensure that all the charred skin is removed. Save the juice remaining in the mixing bowl for the broth in the next step.

4 Boil the water and salt in a saucepan, ensuring that the salt dissolves into the water. Remove the pan from the heat. Add the garlic, parsley, lovage, peppercorns and coriander seeds. Add the leftover liquid from the aubergines and the smoked oil from the tomatoes. Cover with a lid and leave to stand for around 20 minutes. Strain the liquid.

5 Toast the pine nuts, either using a cast-iron pan or a sieve (fine-mesh strainer) above the fire (see tip on page 86).

6 Place a piece of aubergine and 2 Smoked Tomatoes onto each plate. Sprinkle a tablespoon of pine nuts on top. Pour over some broth, add a lemon half and top with parsley leaves.

CHARCOAL-ROASTED SAVOY CABBAGE
with lemon sauce and quail's egg

Serves 6

2 medium heads of savoy cabbage

6 quail's eggs

Lemon sauce

1 tablespoon rapeseed (canola) oil

1 tablespoon finely chopped garlic

1 tablespoon finely chopped shallot

2 tablespoons white wine

3 tablespoons lemon juice

200 g (7 oz/1 cup) unsalted butter, cut into
   small cubes

To serve

3 small green chillies, finely sliced

oregano leaves

oxalis (wood sorrel)

1 Add charcoal or firewood to half of the barbecue (grill) so you have space to roast the cabbage using indirect heat later. Light the barbecue and, once it is burning strongly, place the savoy cabbages straight onto the charcoal so that the outer layer burns. Turn several times using tongs. Pick up the savoy cabbages, place on the grill positioned on the charcoal-free side, close the lid and roast, using indirect heat for around 1 hour until the cabbage feels soft when gently pressed. You can also measure the core temperature – it should be above 80°C (175°F) in the middle.

2 Pour the oil for the lemon sauce into a stainless steel saucepan and put on a medium heat. Add the garlic and shallots and fry until soft, but without taking on any colour. Add the white wine and lemon juice and leave to simmer for around 10 minutes. Strain to remove the shallots, then return the saucepan containing the liquid to the heat and lower the temperature slightly. Add half of the butter and whisk thoroughly until the sauce begins to thicken. Add the rest of the butter and continue whisking until you have a lovely, creamy sauce.

3 Cut the tops off the quail's eggs and carefully pour the contents into the palm of your hand. Allow the egg white to run off and transfer the yolk to your dry hand before passing it back into the eggshell.

4 Remove the outermost burnt cabbage leaves once the cabbages are cool enough to handle. Then cut them into portion-sized pieces. Plate up the cabbage pieces and place the egg shells containing the yolk on top. Garnish with the chilli, oregano and oxalis. Serve the sauce alongside or drizzle it over the cabbage.

CHARCOAL-ROASTED LEEK with calypso beans, smoked onions and fennel broth

Serves 6

3 large leeks

150 g (5 oz/2½ cups) cooked kidney beans

4 Smoked Onions (page 208)

Fennel broth

2 tablespoons rapeseed (canola) oil

1 yellow onion, coarsely chopped with the skin on

1 fennel bulb, coarsely chopped

2 garlic cloves, crushed with the skin on

the green parts of the leeks from above
     (around 200 g/7 oz)

2–3 sprigs of parsley

3 star anise

1 teaspoon white peppercorns

1 teaspoon salt

300 ml (10 fl oz/1¼ cups) water

To serve

fennel flowers or fennel dill

1 Start with the broth. Heat up the oil in a saucepan on a medium heat, add the onion and leave to simmer until it begins to soften. Add the rest of the ingredients except the water and fry while stirring – they should not take on any colour. Pour the water in after around 15 minutes and bring to the boil. Let the broth simmer for around 30 minutes so that it reduces down slightly. Strain and set aside.

2 Add charcoal or firewood to half of the barbecue (grill) so that you have space to roast the leeks using indirect heat later. Light the barbecue and once it is burning strongly, place the leeks straight onto the charcoal so that the outer layer burns. Pick up the leeks, place on the grill and position them on the charcoal-free side. Close the lid and roast using indirect heat for 20–30 minutes until the leeks are soft all the way through. You can measure the core temperature – it should preferably be above 95°C (200°F).

3 Re-heat the broth, add the beans and the Smoked Onions and leave to simmer for a while. Cut the leeks in half and make an incision lengthways on each half. Fill with the beans and broth and garnish with a few fennel flowers.

CHARCOAL-ROASTED RED BEETROOT
with feta and dukkah

Serves 6

6 small red beetroot (beets)

6 slices of sourdough bread

unsalted butter

60 g (2 oz) feta, preferably made
    with goat's milk

6 teaspoons Dukkah (page 204)

fresh mixed herbs, e.g. oregano, parsley,
    shiso and basil

sea salt flakes

1   Add charcoal or firewood to half of the barbecue (grill) so that you have space to roast the beetroot using indirect heat later. Light the barbecue and once it is burning strongly, place the beetroots straight onto the charcoal so that the outer layer burns. Turn several times using tongs. Pick up the beetroots, place on the grill and position them on the charcoal-free side. Close the lid and roast using indirect heat for around 1 hour until the beetroots feel soft when you gently press the skin. You can measure the core temperature – it should preferably be above 85°C (185°F).

2   Peel the beetroots once they are cool enough to handle without burning yourself. It can be a little tricky to remove the skin – try pulling it off with your fingers; otherwise, cut it off with a knife.

3   Let the barbecue get really hot so you can toast the bread. Butter the slices of bread then grill them quickly on the side without butter, turn them over onto the buttered side and grill until there are clear grill stripes.

4   Slice the beetroot and crumble some feta on top. Place them on the grill briefly so that the cheese begins to melt.

5   Place a few slices of beetroot with feta onto each slice of toast, sprinkle some Dukkah over them and top with herbs and sea salt flakes.

CHARCOAL-ROASTED SWEET POTATO
with creamed white beans

Serves 6

6 medium sweet potatoes

Creamed white beans with goat's cheese

2 tablespoons unsalted butter

40 g (1½ oz) finely chopped shallots

1 tablespoon finely chopped garlic

1 tablespoon white wine vinegar

600 g (1 lb 5 oz/3 cups) large white beans, cooked

1 teaspoon finely grated unwaxed lemon zest

200 ml (7 fl oz/scant 1 cup) Vegetable Stock,
   (page 196)

200 ml (7 fl oz/scant 1 cup) double (heavy) cream

100 g (3½ oz) soft goat's cheese (chèvre)

To serve

parsley

olive oil

sea salt flakes and black pepper

1. Light the barbecue (grill). Pierce the sweet potatoes in a few places using a cocktail stick (toothpick) then place them straight onto the glowing charcoal. This can even be done while the charcoal is still burning. Roast the sweet potatoes until the skin has charred completely and they are soft inside, around 20 minutes. Set aside to cool.

2. Dollop the butter into a saucepan and put on a medium heat. Add the shallots and garlic and fry until soft without taking on any colour. Add the vinegar and stir a few times. Add the beans and lemon zest, continue to stir until everything is thoroughly combined. Add the Vegetable Stock, cream and goat's cheese, reduce the heat slightly and leave to simmer until the cheese has completely melted.

3. Cut a lengthways incision into the sweet potatoes. Hollow them out, keeping as much of the brown flesh inside the skin as possible without taking too much of the charred skin. Set aside.

4. Pour the creamy beans into bowls, generously spoon the sweet potatoes over these and top with parsley, olive oil, salt and pepper.

EXPEDITIONARY STORES **This is one of the dishes I love to take out into the woods with me. Fill a vacuum flask with the creamy beans and bring a raw sweet potato for the camp fire.**

05

WOOD-FIRED OVEN

LEVE'S PIZZA DOUGH

Makes 6 pizzas

1 kg (2 lb 4 oz/8 cups) strong flour
700 ml (24 fl oz/scant 3 cups) + 70 ml (2½ fl oz/
    5 tablespoons) water at 40°C (100°F)
200 g (7 oz) active sourdough starter
4 teaspoons sea salt flakes

1 Mix the flour, 700 ml (24 fl oz/scant 3 cups) of water and sourdough starter by hand in a mixing bowl until the temperature of the dough falls to 30–33°C (86–91°F). Cover in cling film (plastic wrap) and leave to rest for 30 minutes. Add the salt and knead it into the dough together with 70 ml (2½ fl oz/5 tablespoons) of water. Leave to prove at room temperature for 1 hour. Fold the dough once every 20 minutes while proving: moisten your hand and pick up the dough's outer edge, pull it carefully and fold it towards the middle. Continue until you have gone all the way around.

2 Leave the dough in the refrigerator for 24 hours. During that time, the dough should increase in volume by 30–50 per cent and feel airy, bubbly and lively. Place the dough on a floured baking board. Divide into roughly 300 g (10½ oz) pieces. Shape the pieces of dough into small balls, but take care not to press too much air out of them. Sprinkle a little flour on each ball, cover them with a dish towel and then in cling film (plastic wrap). Leave them to prove at room temperature for 1–2 hours.

3 When the dough balls have finished proving they should have slackened, sunk and increased in size by around 20 per cent. If you carefully push a finger into the dough and leave a small mark, the dough is ready to be made into pizzas.

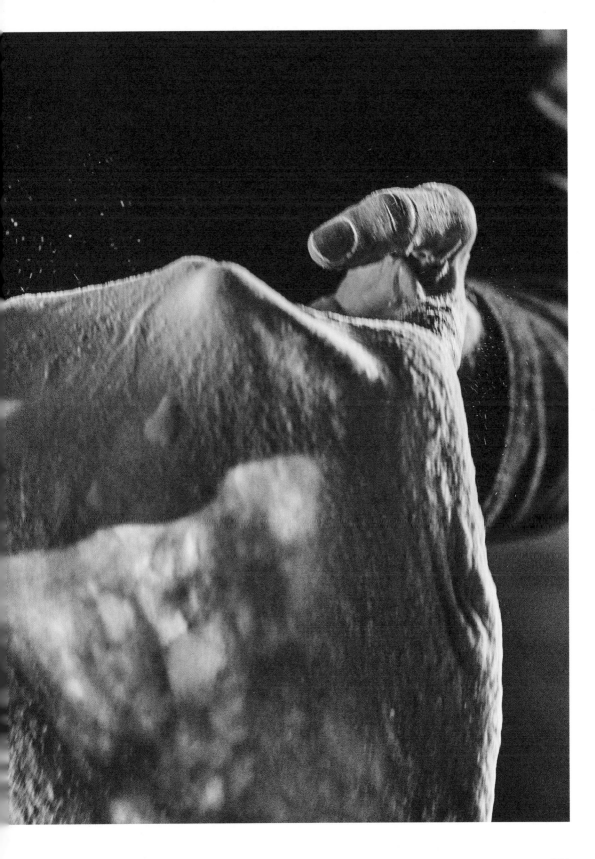

A wood oven is a very special way to bake pizzas and flatbreads. It is also great for roasting vegetables quickly to give them a crispy edge – for example, the Jerusalem artichokes on page 169. These days, you can get hold of amazing small wood ovens with stone bases that reach the perfect heat and can easily climb to over 400°C (800°F).

PIZZA with asparagus, pimientos de Padrón, roasted buckwheat and dill oil

Serves 6

6 balls of Pizza Dough (page 150)

6 small silver onions, chopped

3 tablespoons rapeseed (canola) oil

100 ml (3½ fl oz/scant ½ cup) white wine

30 asparagus spears

6 tablespoons crème fraîche

180 g (6½ oz) mozzarella

6 mild green chillies, e.g. pimientos de Padrón,
   finely sliced

To serve

olive oil

6 tablespoons Roasted Buckwheat,
   (page 206)

1 Heat the wood oven to the highest possible temperature – 350–400°C (660–800°F) is perfect. Leave for a while to ensure that the stone is really hot.

2 Place the onions in a cold saucepan. Add the oil and place the pan on a medium heat. The onions will soon start to release liquid and the flavours will be concentrated through the onions cooking in their own juices. Stir once every 5 minutes for 15–20 minutes. Take care to ensure that the onions don't take on colour or burn to the bottom of the pan. Add the wine and reduce for around 15 minutes until almost all the liquid is gone. Set aside and leave to cool.

3 Cut the tops off the asparagus spears and cut the rest into slices around 5 mm (¼ in) thick.

4 Dust a large chopping board generously with flour. Take a ball of Pizza Dough, shape it into a round pizza and leave it to rest for a few minutes. Dust the pizza paddle with flour and place the pizza base on the paddle while pulling gently at the edges to stretch it out further.

5 Take 1 tablespoon of crème fraîche and spread it out from the middle of the pizza base towards the edge in a thin layer. Tear the mozzarella and place small pieces across the pizza, around 30 g (1 oz) per pizza.

6 Add a thin layer of onions, asparagus and chillies, and put the pizza in the oven. Once the edges of the pizza have bubbled up and taken on a good colour – preferably a little burnt in places – it is ready. Remove the pizza from the oven and brush the crusts with olive oil, then top with a tablespoon of Roasted Buckwheat.

PIZZA with sweet potato, yellow tomato sauce and Belper Knolle

Serves 6

6 balls of Pizza Dough (page 150)

1 sweet potato

1 garlic clove

3 tablespoons unsalted butter, melted

6 tablespoons crème fraîche

2 burrata (weighing 240 g/9 oz)

To serve

marjoram

200 ml (7 fl oz/scant 1 cup) Fermented Yellow
    Tomato Sauce (page 200)

sea salt flakes

Belper Knolle or another hard cheese
    such as Parmesan

1   Heat the wood oven to the highest temperature possible – 350–400°C (660–800°F) is perfect. Leave for a while to ensure that the stone is really hot.

2   Brush and wash the sweet potato. Dry it carefully and cut it as thinly as possible, into slices 1–2 mm ($\frac{1}{16}$ in) thick – use a mandoline if you have one. Place the slices into a bowl, grate the garlic over them, add the melted butter and massage it in using your hands.

3   Dust a large chopping board generously with flour. Take a ball of Pizza Dough, shape it into a round pizza and leave it to rest for a few minutes. Dust the pizza paddle with flour and place the pizza base on the paddle while pulling gently at the edges to stretch it out further.

4   Take 1 tablespoon of crème fraîche and spread it out from the middle of the pizza base towards the edge in a thin layer. Tear the burrata and place small pieces across the pizza, around 40 g (1½ oz) per pizza.

5   Add the slices of sweet potato (save the garlic butter) and put the pizza in the oven. Once the edges of the pizza have bubbled up and taken on a good colour – preferably a little burnt in places – it is ready. Remove the pizza from the oven and brush the crusts with garlic butter, then top with marjoram, 2–3 tablespoons of the Fermented Yellow Tomato Sauce, salt and shavings of Belper Knolle.

PIZZA with figs, hazelnuts and black garlic dressing

Serves 6

6 balls of Pizza Dough (page 150)

6 figs

180 g (6½ oz) hazelnuts (filberts)

6 tablespoons crème fraîche

240 g (8 oz) soft goat's cheese

Dressing

1 vanilla pod (bean)

2 black garlic cloves

4 tablespoons olive oil

2 tablespoons apple cider vinegar

1 tablespoon honey

sea salt flakes

To serve

olive oil

1 Start with the dressing. Cut the vanilla pod lengthways and scrape out the seeds. Place the vanilla seeds together with the other ingredients in a bowl and blend using a hand-held blender or food processor. Set aside.

2 Heat the wood oven to the highest temperature possible – 350–400°C (660–800°F) is perfect. Leave for a while to ensure that the stone is really hot.

3 Cut the figs into thin slices, around 3–4 mm (⅛ in) thick. Halve the hazelnuts.

4 Dust a large chopping board generously with flour. Take each ball of Pizza Dough, shape it into a round pizza and leave it to rest for a few minutes. Dust the pizza paddle with flour and place the pizza base on the paddle while pulling gently at the edges to stretch it out further.

5 Take 1 tablespoon of crème fraîche and spread it out from the middle of each pizza base towards the edge in a thin layer. Place small chunks of goat's cheese on top, around 40 g (1½ oz) per pizza.

6 Add fig slices and the halved hazelnuts, and put each pizza in turn in the oven. Once the edges of the pizzas have bubbled up and taken on a good colour, even a little burnt in places, they are ready. Remove from the oven and brush the crusts with olive oil and drizzle a tablespoon of dressing on top.

PIZZA with pumpkin and chanterelles

Serves 6

6 balls of Pizza Dough (page 150)

1 small Uchiki Kuri pumpkin (winter squash)
   or butternut squash

1 garlic clove

2 tablespoons olive oil

6 tablespoons crème fraîche

240 g (8 oz) soft goat's cheese (chèvre)

180 g (6 oz) chanterelles

To serve

oregano

oxalis (wood sorrel) (preferably with flowers)

sea salt flakes

1   Heat the wood oven to the highest temperature possible – 350–400°C (660–800°F) is perfect. Leave for a while to ensure that the stone is really hot.

2   Peel the squash and cut into thin slices, preferably using a mandoline. Place the slices into a bowl, grate the garlic over them, add the oil and massage it in using your hands.

3   Dust a large chopping board generously with flour. Take a ball of Pizza Dough, shape it into a round pizza and leave it to rest for a few minutes. Dust the pizza paddle with flour and place the pizza base on the paddle while pulling gently at the edges to stretch it out further.

4   Take 1 tablespoon of crème fraîche and spread it out from the middle of the pizza base towards the edge in a thin layer. Place small chunks of goat's cheese on top, around 40 g (1½ oz) per pizza.

5   Add a few slices of squash (saving the garlic oil) and mushrooms. Put the pizza in the hot oven. When the pizza's edges have bubbled up and taken on a good colour – preferably a little burned in places – it is ready. Remove from the oven and brush the crusts with garlic oil. Garnish with oregano, oxalis and salt. Repeat with the remaining dough balls.

MAXIMISE HEAT **Regardless of whether you have access to a wood oven or a normal oven, the trick is to get it to the highest temperature possible and to use some kind of flat stone to bake the pizza on. I use a wood oven from Ooni that is good value and easy to use. But there are plenty of other ways to bake pizza – including a normal barbecue (grill), so use trial and error to find the best option for you.**

PIZZA with blue potatoes, Brussels sprouts and truffle

Serves 6

6 balls of Pizza Dough (page 150)

6 small blue potatoes

1 garlic clove

3 tablespoons unsalted butter, melted

6 tablespoons crème fraîche

180 g (6½ oz) mozzarella

180 g (6½ oz) pecorino

12 Brussels sprouts

To serve

fresh truffle

1   Heat the wood oven to the highest temperature possible – 350–400°C (660–800°F) is perfect. Leave for a while to ensure that the stone is really hot.

2   Brush and wash the potatoes. Dry them carefully and cut them as thinly as possible into slices 1–2 mm (¹⁄₁₆ in) thick – use a mandoline if you can. Place the slices into a bowl, grate the garlic over them, add the melted butter and massage it in using your hands.

3   Dust a large chopping board generously with flour. Take a ball of Pizza Dough, shape it into a round pizza and leave it to rest for a few minutes. Dust the pizza paddle with flour and place the pizza base on the paddle while pulling gently at the edges to stretch it out further.

4   Take 1 tablespoon of crème fraîche and spread it out from the middle of the pizza base towards the edge in a thin layer. Tear the mozzarella and place small pieces across the pizza, around 30 g (1 oz) per pizza. Crumble the pecorino into small pieces and spread across the pizza, around 30 g (1 oz) on each.

5   Add a few slices of potato, finely slice the Brussels sprouts and sprinkle on top, then put the pizza in the oven. Once the edges of the pizza have bubbled up and taken on a good colour – preferably a little burnt in places – it is ready. Remove the pizza from the oven and brush the crusts with the garlic butter and garnish with shavings of truffle. Repeat with the remaining dough balls.

FLATBREAD with carrots and sage

Serves 6

300 ml (10 fl oz/1¼ cups) kefir (or filmjölk)

2 teaspoons dried yeast

1 egg

2 tablespoons rapeseed (canola) oil

1 tablespoon honey

1 teaspoon salt

400 g (14 oz/3¼ cups) plain (all-purpose) flour

½ teaspoon baking powder

Topping

2 purple carrots, peeled

2 yellow carrots, peeled

2 garlic cloves

3 tablespoons ghee or melted unsalted butter

sage

sea salt flakes

1 Take the kefir out of the refrigerator well in advance so that it is close to room temperature. Place the dried yeast in a mixing bowl and whisk in the kefir so that the yeast dissolves. Add the egg, oil, honey and salt and whisk until smooth.

2 Mix together the flour and baking powder in a bowl. Gradually add it a little at a time to the kefir and knead into a smooth dough for 7 minutes using a dough hook. The dough should come away from the edges of the bowl and not stick. The quantity of flour can vary, so make sure you have a little extra on hand.

3 Cover the dough with a clean dish towel and leave to prove for 1–1½ hours, or until the dough has doubled in size.

4 Divide the dough into six pieces and shape into round balls by folding in the edges towards the middle so that you have a nice surface tension. Place the balls on a floured baking sheet with the joint facing down and press them gently with the palm of your hand. Cover with a dish towel and leave them to prove for another hour.

5 Heat the oven to the highest possible temperature – 350–400°C (660–800°F) is perfect. Leave for a while to ensure that the stone is really hot.

6 Dust a large chopping board generously with flour. Take a dough ball and flatten it into a circle. Work it with a rolling pin in one direction so that the bread becomes an oval shape and leave the dough to rest for a few minutes. Dust the pizza paddle with flour and place the flatbread on the paddle while pulling gently at the edges to make it slightly more taut.

7 Cut the peeled carrots lengthways into thin slices. Grate the garlic into the ghee and brush over the bread. Distribute the carrot slices and sage leaves evenly across the bread. Brush again with the garlic ghee and top with a little sea salt.

8 Put in the oven and bake for around 1½ minutes or until the edges take on a lovely, golden yellow, with a slightly burnt tone. Repeat with the remaining dough balls.

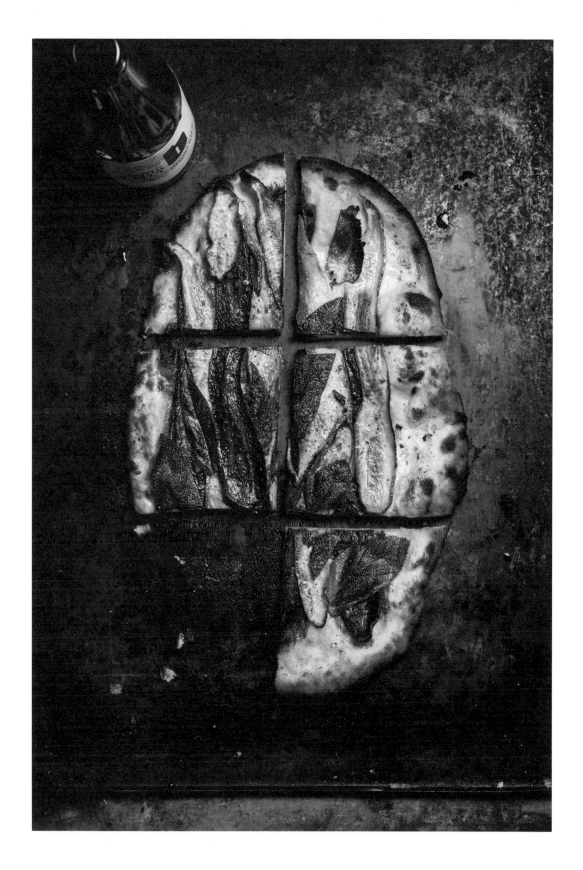

WOOD OVEN ROASTED CARROTS
with labneh

Serves 6

1 litre (34 fl oz/4 cups) plain yoghurt

12 medium purple carrots

100 ml (3½ fl oz/scant ½ cup) apple brandy,
    e.g. calvados

1 tablespoon honey

2 tablespoons rapeseed (canola) oil

sea salt flakes

1 Put a funnel with a coffee filter paper in it into a jug and pour in the yoghurt. Leave in the refrigerator for 24 hours. When you take it out, you should have around 500 ml (17 fl oz/2 cups) of whey in the jug and a thick, creamy labneh in the filter paper.

2 Light your wood oven or set your oven to its highest temperature, around 230°C (450°F/ Gas 10).

3 Soak the carrots for a while to remove most of the soil and gravel. Remove them from the water and scrub them gently with a root vegetable brush to remove anything else. Use a small vegetable knife to scrape around the base of the leaves to remove all the soil bacteria. Dry the carrots carefully with a dish (tea) towel and set to one side.

4 Put a frying pan (skillet) on a medium heat. Pour in the yoghurt whey and bring to the boil. Add the carrots and cook them for 10–15 minutes until they are soft on the outside.

5 Remove the carrots, but let the whey continue to cook in the pan. Let the carrots steam until dry and then put them in a baking tray (pan).

6 Pour the apple brandy and honey into the whey. Raise the heat slightly and cook until it has reduced to one sixth of the volume while stirring constantly – this will take around 15–20 minutes. Remove from the heat and set to one side.

7 Drizzle the rapeseed oil and sprinkle the sea salt flakes over the carrots and then put them in the wood oven. Remove them after 1–2 minutes, shake the baking tray and then return it to the oven. Repeat this four times. Remove the carrots from the oven and then leave to rest.

8 Put a large spoonful of labneh and two carrots onto each plate. Drizzle a couple of spoonfuls of the whey reduction on top.

JERUSALEM ARTICHOKE SOUP
made with smoked buttermilk

Serves 6

600 g (1 lb 5 oz) Jerusalem artichokes

6-7 garlic cloves, crushed with the skins on

1 sprig of thyme

1 sprig of oregano

3 tablespoons rapeseed (canola) oil

sea salt flakes

Soup base

1 tablespoon Smoked Butter (page 178)

1 tablespoon rapeseed (canola) oil

70 g (2½ oz) finely chopped shallots

400 ml (13 fl oz/generous 1½ cups) dry
   apple cider

200 ml (7 fl oz/scant 1 cup) Vegetable Stock,
   (page 196)

400 ml (13 fl oz/generous 1½ cups) Smoked
   Buttermilk (page 178)

To serve

6 tablespoons melted Smoked Butter,
   (page 178)

watercress

sea salt flakes and black pepper

1 Light the wood oven and let it reach a temperature of around 250°C (480°F).

2 Wash and scrub the Jerusalem artichokes thoroughly. Dry them completely using a dish (tea) towel and then put them on a baking sheet together with the garlic and herbs. Drizzle with oil and sprinkle some sea salt flakes on top before putting the sheet in the oven. Remove it after 4–5 minutes, shake the baking sheet and then return it to the oven. Repeat this four times.

Remove the baking sheet and cover with kitchen foil so that the artichokes continue to steam and cook in their own heat. Leave them to stand for 10–15 minutes. Cut one third of the Jerusalem artichokes into slices 5 mm (¼ in) thick and set aside. Hollow out the rest and use for the soup base. You should be left with 300 g (10½ oz) flesh from the Jerusalem artichokes.

3 Mix the Smoked Butter and oil in a cold saucepan. Add the shallots and then put the pan on a medium heat. Stir constantly using a wooden spoon and let the shallots soften without taking on any colour, around 10 minutes. Pour over the apple cider, raise the heat and leave to cook for another 5 minutes. Add the Vegetable Stock, Smoked Buttermilk and the Jerusalem artichoke flesh. Reduce the heat, whisk thoroughly so that everything is properly mixed and then leave to simmer for a further 10 minutes. Remove from the heat, cover with a lid and set aside.

4 Place a small heap of sliced Jerusalem artichokes in each dish and distribute the soup between the dishes. Drizzle a little melted Smoked Butter over each bowl and top with watercress, salt and pepper.

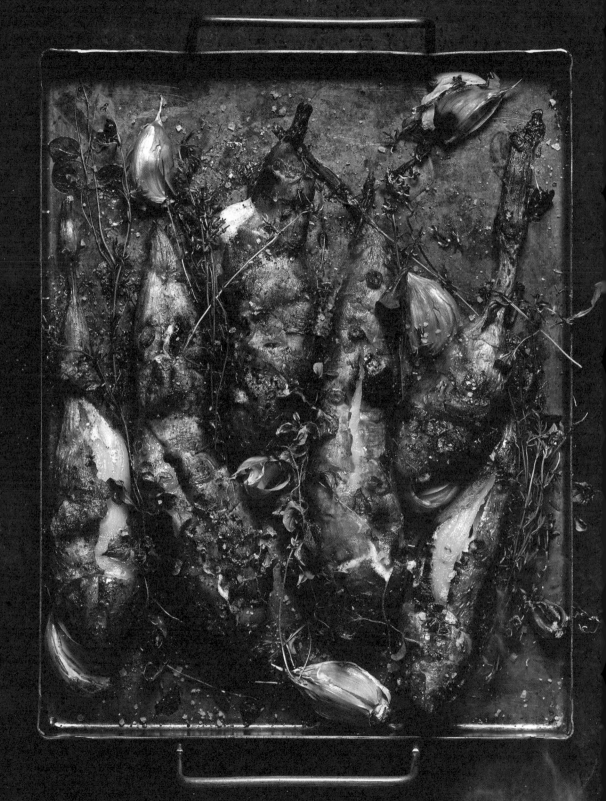

WOOD OVEN ROASTED CHESTNUTS
with asparagus and smoked cream

Serves 6

600 g (1 lb 5 oz) asparagus spears

2 tablespoons rapeseed (canola) oil

400 g (14 oz) whole chestnuts

2 tablespoons melted unsalted butter

sea salt flakes

To serve

200 ml (7 fl oz/scant 1 cup) Smoked Cream,
    (page 178)

½ unwaxed lime

nasturtiums, leaves and flowers, or watercress

sea salt flakes

1   Light the wood oven and let it reach a temperature of around 300°C (575°F).

2   Trim and wash the asparagus spears. Dry them and place them in a bowl together with a tablespoon of the oil. Mix so that everything is covered in oil.

3   Score a cross in the top of each chestnut. Put them in a cast-iron pan, drizzle a tablespoon of rapeseed oil over, sprinkle with some sea salt flakes and put them in the wood oven. Remove after 1–2 minutes, shake the pan then return it to the oven. Repeat this four times. Remove the chestnuts from the oven and leave to rest.

4   Place the asparagus in a cast-iron pan and put it in the oven. Remove from the oven after around 1 minute – they cook quickly so keep an eye on them. Shake the pan or turn the asparagus over and return to the oven for another minute. Once done, remove the asparagus and set aside.

5   Peel the chestnuts and put them in a bowl with the melted butter and stir. Remove the chestnuts after a few minutes and set aside. Pour the Smoked Cream into the bowl and grate the lime peel over the top. Whisk so that the cream and butter combine.

6   Pour 2–3 tablespoons of the Smoked Cream onto each plate and place the chestnuts and asparagus on top. Garnish with nasturtiums and a pinch of salt.

05 WOOD-FIRED OVEN

173

06

SMOKED
AND
SOURED

SMOKED CREAM

700 ml (24 fl oz/scant 3 cups) double
   (heavy) cream
glowing charcoal

1 Light the barbecue (grill) with wood so that
   there is a strong glow.
2 Pour the cream into a heatproof container.
   Select a glowing piece of charcoal by eye and
   pick it up with tongs. Put the charcoal in
   the cream and leave it there for a few hours,
   preferably overnight in the refrigerator.
3 Strain through a coarse meshed strainer and
   store in a lidded container in the refrigerator
   until needed.

SMOKED BUTTER AND BUTTERMILK

700 ml (24 fl oz/scant 3 cups) Smoked Cream,
   see adjacent recipe
sea salt flakes

1 Whisk the Smoked Cream until it turns
   to butter. How long this takes depends
   on which method you use, but you will be
   able to clearly tell when it is ready. The
   liquid that gathers around the lump of
   butter is the smoked buttermilk – keep it,
   stored in a lidded container in the refrigerator
   – it is great for cooking with vegetables and
   legumes.
2 Rinse the lump of butter under cold water
   and let the last of the liquid drain. Put the
   butter in a dish towel and dry it carefully,
   ensuring you remove the liquid on the
   surface. Salt thoroughly and store in an
   airtight container in the refrigerator.

COLD SOUR TOMATO SOUP

Serves 6

1.5 litres (50 fl oz/6 cups) Fermented Yellow
    Tomato Sauce (page 200)
360 ml (12 fl oz/1½ cups) gin (60 ml/2 fl oz/
    ¼ cup per portion)
a few drops of habanero sauce (optional)

Kohlrabi in elderflower vinegar

2 small kohlrabi
100 ml (3½ fl oz/scant ½ cup) elderflower vinegar,
    or Champagne vinegar or apple cider vinegar
small pinch of sea salt flakes

To serve

Smoked Tomatoes + a little of the oil,
    (page 208)
multigrain crackers
elderflowers (optional)

1 Peel and dice the kohlrabi into bite-sized pieces. Put the cubes of kohlrabi in a bowl then add the vinegar and salt and leave to soak for around 1 hour.

2 Thoroughly mix the Fermented Yellow Tomato Sauce with the gin and habanero sauce in a large jug. Chill before serving.

3 Pour around 300 ml (10 fl oz/1¼ cups) of soup into each bowl, add 3–4 Smoked Tomatoes and drizzle a little of the smoked oil on top. Finish with 2 tablespoons of kohlrabi cubes, multigrain crackers and elderflowers, if they are in season.

COLDER SOUP **Personally, I like my soup at refrigerator temperature, but you can also add a few ice cubes if you would like an even more cooling dish on a hot summer's day.**

Saw a deep cross into a big piece of wood as this can function as a hearth and grill. Ignite some sawdust in the bottom of the cross and let it burn along the piece of wood until you have a nice glow. It will burn for several hours.

SMOKY ONION SOUP with white mould cheese gratin

Serves 6

12 medium yellow onions, finely chopped

4 tablespoons unsalted butter

1 tablespoon white wine vinegar

1 teaspoon salt

500 ml (17 fl oz/2 cups) white wine

500 ml (17 fl oz/2 cups) Vegetable Stock,
   (page 196)

Baked white mould cheese

1 white mould cheese, e.g. Camembert,
   preferably in a wooden box

1 garlic clove, quartered

1 sprig of rosemary

2 tablespoons white wine

To serve

toasted bread

thyme

1 Set fire to a few pieces of firewood in a barbecue (grill) with a lid then place the grill on top, or set fire to sawdust in a large, sawn piece of wood (page 183).

2 Mix the onions, butter, vinegar and salt in a cold, wet terrine dish. Place over the flames and cover with a lid. The onions will soon start to release liquid and the flavours will be concentrated through the onions cooking in their own juices. Stir using a wooden spoon every 15 minutes. Take care to make sure it does not burn. (If you notice that it is getting too dry, you can add the wine a little earlier.) Every time you stir it, circle the lid above the terrine so that the smoke wafts into the pot and flavours the onions.

3 Pour in the wine and Vegetable Stock after about 1 hour and leave to simmer for a further 2–3 hours, depending on temperature. The onions should be a dark brown colour and the liquid should have reduced by at least a quarter. Check the terrine occasionally and circle the lid to add more smoke.

4 Remove from the heat and add new charcoal or wood to one side of the barbecue and light. If you have a barbecue thermometer, the temperature should be around 200°C (400°F). Put the cheese in its wooden box in a baking tray (it may leak slightly so it's good to have a container to catch this). Score a cross in the cheese and insert the garlic. Add a small sprig of rosemary and pour the wine over. Put the baking tray on the grill, close the lid and let it bake using indirect heat for around 20 minutes. At the same time, toast the bread on the grill above the glowing charcoal.

5 Serve the onion soup in bowls, topped with sprigs of thyme, alongside the cheese in its tray. Dip the toast in the cheese and spoon the onions on top.

ENSURE SUCCESS WITH ONIONS **When I cut up onions to cook them for a long time, I want the pieces to be as even as possible. I start by cutting off the root and top of the onion before halving them lengthways from root to top. Then I peel the onion and continue to cut in the same direction into pieces as evenly sized as possible, around 3–4 mm (⅛ in) thick.**

SMOKY BEETROOT AND MUSHROOM STEW

Serves 6

3 red beetroot (beets)

3 yellow beetroot (beets)

2 tablespoons rapeseed (canola) oil

300 g (10½ oz) mixed mushrooms, cut into
   generous pieces

3 yellow onions, peeled and quartered

2 garlic cloves, crushed with the skin on

1 bay leaf

1 sprig of thyme

1 tablespoon red wine vinegar

600 ml (20 fl oz/2½ cups) red wine

400 ml (13 fl oz/generous 1½ cups) Vegetable
   Stock (page 196)

To serve

thyme

parsley

1 tablespoon rapeseed (canola) oil, preferably
   flavoured with thyme

sea salt flakes and black pepper

Quick-pickled Baby Onions (page 211)

1   Add charcoal or firewood to half the barbecue (grill) so that you have space to roast the beetroots using indirect heat later. Light the barbecue and once it is burning strongly, place the beetroots straight onto the charcoal so that the outer layer burns. Turn several times using tongs. Place the grill on high and then position the beetroots away from the flames. Close the lid and roast using indirect heat for 1 hour until the beetroots feel soft when you gently press the skin. You can measure the core temperature – it should be above 90°C (195°F). Remove from the grill and leave to cool.

2   Continue with the next step while the beetroots are roasting. Set fire to a few pieces of firewood in a barbecue with a lid and then place the grill on top, or set fire to sawdust in a large, sawn piece of wood (page 183).

3   Pour oil into a wet terrine dish and position above the flames. Add the mushrooms when the oil begins to smoke and let them take on colour, stirring occasionally. Remove using a slotted spoon and set aside.

4   Put the onions into the oil and fry until they begin to soften and take on colour, for around 5 minutes. Add the garlic cloves, bay leaf and thyme and stir a few times. Add the vinegar and wait for 1 minute for it to be fried off and absorbed by the onions, stirring constantly to stop it from burning. Pour in the wine and Vegetable Stock and leave to simmer for 1 hour. Check the liquid occasionally to see it is not boiling away, stirring when you do. When opening the lid, circle it above the terrine so that smoke wafts into the pot and flavours it. Strain the stock into another container and clean the terrine.

5   Peel the beetroots once they have cooled slightly. Try pulling the skin off using your fingers, otherwise cut it off using a knife. Cut the beetroots into generous pieces that can be eaten using a spoon.

6   Place the terrine back over the glowing charcoal, add the mushrooms and beetroots. Pour the stock over and bring back to the boil. Remove from the heat and tear in some thyme and parsley. Top with the oil and season with salt and pepper to taste. Serve alongside a bowl of the Quick-pickled Baby Onions.

07

BUNS, SIDES AND CONDIMENTS

SWEET POTATO BUNS

For 10–12 buns

50 g (2 oz/¼ cup) butter

250 ml (8½ fl oz/1 cup) whole (full-fat) milk

15–20 g (½–1 oz) fresh yeast

2 tablespoons sugar

1 teaspoons salt

1 egg

200 g (7 oz) boiled sweet potatoes

650 g (1 lb 7 oz/4⅓ cups) plain
  (all-purpose) flour

1 egg + 1 tablespoons water for brushing

sesame seeds

1   Melt the butter over a low heat, then add the milk. Heat to body temperature – approx. 37°C (99°F). Crumble the yeast into a bowl. Pour the milk into the bowl and stir so that the yeast dissolves. Whisk in the sugar, salt and egg.

2   Boil the peeled sweet potatoes until soft, mash with a fork and stir the mash into the contents of the bowl.

3   Mix in the flour a little at a time. Knead the dough for about 5 minutes in a stand mixer with a dough hook or for 10 minutes by hand. It should be elastic and easy to work, and should fall away from the edges easily.

4   Cover the dough with a tea (dish) towel. Leave in a warm place to rise for about 1½–2 hours, or until it has doubled in size.

5   Divide the dough into 10–12 pieces and shape into round balls by folding the edges in towards the middle, so you achieve good surface tension – pretty much like taking an opened flower and folding the petals together to form a bud again. Put the buns on a baking tray lined with baking parchment, with the seam facing downwards, and gently press them with the palm of your hand. Cover with a tea towel and allow them to rise for a further 45 minutes.

6   Preheat the oven to 200°C (400°F/Gas 6).

7   Whisk the egg with 1 tablespoon of water. Brush the tops of the buns with the beaten egg and sprinkle a few sesame seeds over them.

8   Put the buns in the oven and reduce the heat to 180°C (350°F/Gas 4). Bake for 10–15 minutes, depending on size. Take a bun out after 10 minutes and tap the bottom – if it sounds hollow it is done. Allow to cool on a cooling rack and store in a ziplock bag or airtight container.

CHARCOAL BUNS

For 10–12 buns:

Ingredients for Sweet Potato Buns (page 192)
15 g (½ oz) active charcoal powder (page 233)

Follow the recipe for the sweet potato buns, but add the charcoal powder when you add the milk. Thoroughly stir in the charcoal powder.

You can find active charcoal in health food shops and on the internet. Apart from giving you the most amazing jet-black buns, charcoal is said to be good for your health.

VEGETABLE STOCK

Makes about 2 litres (68 fl oz/8 cups)

2 tablespoons rapeseed (canola) oil

140 g (5 oz) coarsely chopped yellow onion

80 g (3 oz) coarsely chopped leek

50 g (2 oz) coarsely chopped carrot

100 g (3½ oz) coarsely chopped celery stalks

40 g (1½ oz) coarsely chopped fennel

1 whole garlic, halved and crushed

2 bay leaves

1 teaspoon white peppercorns

1 teaspoon coriander seeds

1 tablespoon white wine vinegar

4 litres (140 fl oz/16 cups) water

6 sprigs of parsley

4 sprigs of lovage

1 Pour the oil into a large saucepan and put on a medium heat. Add all the ingredients except the water, parsley and lovage and stir until everything is thoroughly mixed. Fry until the vegetables soften; this usually takes 5–7 minutes. Stir occasionally so that the vegetables do not take on too much colour.

2 Raise the heat, add the water and cook until the stock has reduced in volume by around half, after about 1–1½ hours.

3 Remove the pan from the heat. Add the parsley and lovage and leave covered for another 20–30 minutes. Strain the stock into a mixing bowl and keep in the refrigerator or pour into an ice cube tray and freeze.

PICKLED RED ONIONS

salt

500 g (1 lb 2 oz) red onions, finely sliced

Spicy 1-2-3 syrup

200 ml (7 fl oz/scant 1 cup) vinegar, preferably 12 per cent

330 g (11 fl oz/1⅔ cups) caster (superfine) sugar or cane sugar

600 ml (20 fl oz/2½ cups) water

3 coriander roots, finely chopped

2–4 bird's eye chillies

2 bay leaves

1 teaspoon black peppercorns

1 teaspoon coriander seeds

1 teaspoon pink peppercorns

1 Start with the syrup. Boil the vinegar, sugar and water in a pan, stirring until the sugar has dissolved. Add the herbs and spices, reduce the heat and leave to simmer for a few minutes. Strain the syrup and leave to cool, ideally leave it in the refrigerator so that it cools completely.

2 Boil a pan of water with plenty of salt. Add the onions and blanch for around 2 minutes. Pour the onions into a colander and rinse with cold water until they are cold. Place the onions into a mixing bowl with cold water and ice cubes.

3 Drain the onions and put in a glass jar. Pour in the syrup and put the jar in the refrigerator. The pickled onions will be ready after 24 hours.

TOMATO KETCHUP

Makes 500 ml (17 fl oz/2 cups)

1 kg (2 lb 3 oz) plum tomatoes

sea salt and freshly ground black pepper

1 pinch of ground cinnamon

1 pinch of ground allspice

1 pinch of ground cloves

1 teaspoon coriander seeds

2 teaspoons grated fresh ginger

2 teaspoons onion powder

2 teaspoons paprika powder

2 tablespoons apple cider vinegar

1 tablespoon sherry vinegar

1 tablespoon honey

200 ml (7 fl oz/scant 1 cup) water

1 Preheat the oven to 140°C (275°F/Gas 1).

2 Halve the tomatoes and lay them on a baking tray (pan) lined with baking parchment, with the cut surfaces uppermost. Sprinkle them with salt and pepper, and bake in the middle of the oven for 2 hours.

3 Bring the baked tomatoes and remaining ingredients to the boil in a heavy-based saucepan. Then reduce the heat and simmer for about 30 minutes.

4 Remove the saucepan from the heat and blend the contents with a hand blender until smooth, then pass the tomato mixture through a fine-mesh sieve (using a spoon to press out as much of the mixture as possible).

5 Wash the saucepan and pour the tomato sauce back into it. Bring the tomato sauce to the boil again and cook for about 30 minutes to reduce to a creamy ketchup. The consistency will get creamier when the ketchup cools, so it is a good idea to test it by putting a spoonful on a plate and allowing it to cool to make sure the consistency is good.

6 Pour the ketchup into clean, sterilised glass bottles. Store in the refrigerator.

TRY FLAVOURING THE KETCHUP **with roasted cavolo nero! Finely chop the cavolo nero (page 218) and fold it into 100 g (3½ oz) of tomato ketchup. Then add another 300 g (10½ oz) ketchup and mix well. You can also make a kimchi-spiced ketchup by mixing one part White Kimchi Base (page 200) and two parts ketchup.**

FERMENTED YELLOW TOMATO SAUCE

1 kg (2 lb 4 oz) yellow tomatoes

100 g (3½ oz) celery stalks

24 g (5 teaspoons) salt, without iodine

200 ml (7 fl oz) White Kimchi Base,
    see adjacent recipe

1 large (1.5 litres/50 fl oz/6 cups) sterilised
    clip-top preserving jar with a rubber seal
    (such as a Kilner jar)

1 Rinse and halve the tomatoes. Clean the celery and slice it thinly. Put the tomatoes and celery together in a bowl and massage in the salt. Apply plenty of pressure to the tomatoes so that they release liquid. Leave to stand at room temperature for at least 1 hour. Stir and apply pressure occasionally.

2 Pour the kimchi base into the bowl and mix using your hands.

3 Pour the mixture into the preserving jar, leaving 2–3 cm (1 in) of air at the top. Fill a plastic bag with water, knot the bag and add it on top as a weight. Close the lid and seal with the bracket. Place the jar on a plate and ideally stand it in a plastic bag since it is very likely that some liquid will leak (make sure you don't seal the bag at the top). Leave the jar to stand at room temperature for 5–7 days.

4 Put the jar in the refrigerator. Remove the jar after a few days, pour its contents into a bowl and blend until smooth. Strain the sauce, pour into sterilised bottles and store in the refrigerator.

WHITE KIMCHI BASE

500 ml (17 fl oz/2 cups) water

2 tablespoons rice flour

100 g (3½ oz) light miso paste

4 shallots, coarsely chopped

2 white or yellow medium carrots, coarsely chopped

100 g (3½ oz) coarsely chopped radishes
    (around 3–4 mm)

about 12 g (½ oz) fresh ginger root

50 g (2 oz) coarsely chopped garlic

2 mild white chillies, about 50 g (2 oz),
    e.g. aji pepper

1 Pour the water and rice flour into a saucepan and bring to the boil. Stir constantly to ensure there are no lumps. Reduce the heat and add the miso paste. Stir and leave to simmer for around 5 minutes. Remove the saucepan from the heat and allow to cool. You can leave the mixture in the refrigerator overnight.

2 Add the shallots, carrots, radishes, ginger and garlic to a food processor and mix into a fine purée. If it is stiff you can add a little splash of water.

3 Pour the rice flour mixture, the vegetable purée and chillies into a glass jar and mix thoroughly. Keep in the refrigerator. If you don't intend to use it for a while, you can also freeze it.

MAYONNAISE USING AQUAFABA

100 ml (3½ fl oz/scant ½ cup) aquafaba (water
    from soaking chickpeas/garbanzos)
1 tablespoon Dijon mustard
1 tablespoon lemon juice
500 ml (17 fl oz/2 cups) rapeseed (canola) oil
    (not cold pressed)
salt

1   Put all the ingredients, except the oil,
    in a beaker or a tall, narrow bowl. Mix using
    a hand-held blender until everything is
    blended.
2   Place the hand-held blender so it rests on the
    bottom of the bowl and add the oil in a thin
    stream while mixing (holding the hand-
    held blender still at the bottom of the bowl).
    When you notice the mayonnaise starting to
    settle, pull the hand-held blender upwards.
    Continue mixing to a good consistency and
    season with salt.

MAYONNAISE USING BOILED POTATOES

2 large potatoes, boiled and peeled
    (about 300 g/10½ oz)
2 tablespoons Dijon mustard
1 teaspoon lemon juice
1 teaspoon salt
1 pinch of white pepper

Put all the ingredients in a mixer and mix at full
power for around 1½ minutes.

MAYONNAISE USING EGGS

2 eggs
1 tablespoon Dijon mustard
1 tablespoon white wine vinegar
2 tablespoons cold-pressed olive oil (optional)
500 ml (17 fl oz/2 cups) rapeseed (canola) oil
    (not cold pressed)
sea salt flakes

1   Crack the eggs into a beaker or a tall,
    narrow bowl. Add the Dijon mustard, vinegar
    and olive oil (optional) to add extra flavour.
    Only using cold-pressed olive oil in the
    mayonnaise will make it too bitter – a dash,
    however, will add some bite, especially if the
    mayonnaise is otherwise natural.
2   Mix using a hand-held blender until
    everything is blended. Position the blender
    so it is touching the bottom of the bowl
    and add the rapeseed oil in a thin stream
    while mixing (holding the blender still at
    the bottom of the bowl). When you notice
    the mayonnaise starting to settle, pull the
    blender upwards. Continue mixing to a good
    consistency and season with salt.

SRIRACHA MAYONNAISE **Choose one of the basic recipes above and
add 2 tablespoons of sriracha sauce once you have mixed it together.
Stir in gently.**

THE GREEN BARBECUE COOKBOOK

DUKKAH

60 g (2 oz) hazelnuts (filberts), without shells

8 macadamia nuts

1 teaspoon coriander seeds

½ teaspoon cumin seeds

1 teaspoon mild chilli powder, e.g. piment
    d'Espelette

½ teaspoon dried oregano

1 teaspoon salt

1 Put a dry frying pan (skillet) on a medium heat and add the nuts and coriander seeds. Roast for about 5 minutes until golden-brown. Stir occasionally to ensure they do not burn. Take off the heat.

2 Place in a food processor and add the cumin, chilli, oregano and salt. Run a few blitzes or pulses – it should be in small pieces but not too finely chopped. Store in a dry, airtight container.

CHICORY DUKKAH

3 tablespoons sweet almonds

8 walnuts

1 tablespoon sunflower seeds

1 tablespoon white sesame seeds

1 teaspoon coriander seeds

1 teaspoon nigella seeds

1 teaspoon dried chicory (endive) root

1 teaspoon salt

1 Put a dry frying pan (skillet) on a medium heat and add the nuts, sunflower, sesame and coriander seeds. Roast for about 5 minutes until golden-brown. Stir occasionally to ensure it does not burn. Take off the heat.

2 Place in a food processor and add the nigella seeds, chicory and salt. Run a few blitzes or pulses – it should be in small pieces but not too finely chopped. Store in a dry, airtight container.

BLACK DUKKAH

1 leek

1 slice of dark rye bread (preferably sweetened
    with malt syrup)

50 g (2 oz) walnuts

1 tablespoon black sesame seeds

1 teaspoon coriander seeds

1 teaspoon nigella seeds

1 tablespoon finely chopped ancho chilli

1 teaspoon black Himalaya salt

1 Set the oven to the highest temperature. Cut the leeks into long, thin, flat strips. Place on a baking sheet and put in the oven for a few minutes until they are completely black. Remove the baking sheet and turn the leeks over. Return to the oven and let the other side turn black. Remove and leave to cool. Use a food processor to blitz the leeks into a fine powder.

2 Put a dry frying pan (skillet) on a medium heat. Tear the bread and add it to the pan together with the walnuts, sesame seeds and coriander seeds. Toast until everything takes on a little colour and begins to smell fragrant, around 5 minutes. Stir occasionally to ensure it does not burn. Take off the heat.

3 Put the mixture in a food processor, add the nigella seeds, chilli and salt and run a few blitzes or pulses. It should be in small pieces but not too finely chopped. Store in a dry, airtight container.

FURIKAKE WITH ROASTED BLACK KALE

10 g (½ oz) black kale leaves

2 tablespoons whole buckwheat

2 tablespoons sweet almonds

2 tablespoons sunflower seeds

1 tablespoon black sesame seeds

1 tablespoon white sesame seeds

½ teaspoon Sichuan peppercorns

10 g (½ oz) dried dead man's fingers (or dried nori)

sea salt flakes

1 Set the oven to 120°C (250°F/Gas 1). Place the black kale on a baking sheet and roast until completely dry and crispy, around 20 minutes.

2 Put a dry frying pan (skillet) on a medium heat and add the buckwheat, sweet almonds, sunflower seeds, sesame seeds and Sichuan peppercorns. Toast until beginning to colour and smells fragrant, around 5 minutes. Stir occasionally to ensure it does not burn. Take off the heat.

3 Put the nut mixture in a food processor, crumble in the black kale leaves and seaweed and add a pinch of salt. Run a few blitzes or pulses – it should be in small pieces but not too finely chopped. Store the furikake in a dry, airtight container.

ROASTED BUCKWHEAT

280 g (10 oz / 1⅔ cups) whole buckwheat

1 tablespoon rapeseed (canola) oil

1 Rinse the buckwheat in hot and then cold water. Place in a mixing bowl, fill with water and leave to stand for at least 1 hour.

2 Strain and place the buckwheat on a dish towel and let it dry slightly.

3 Put a frying pan (skillet) on a medium heat, add the oil and let it heat up. Add the buckwheat just before the oil begins to smoke. Fry the buckwheat until it turns crispy and golden brown, around 5 minutes. Stir occasionally to ensure it does not burn.

HARISSA

6 mild red chillies

1 large red (bell) pepper

1 teaspoon sea salt flakes

½ teaspoon coriander seeds

½ teaspoon cumin seeds

½ teaspoon black peppercorns

2 tablespoons rapeseed (canola) oil

100 g (3½ oz) finely chopped red onion

3 garlic cloves, finely chopped

1½ tablespoons tomato purée (paste)

2 tablespoons lemon juice

1 teaspoon salt

1 Light the barbecue (grill) and while the fire is still burning grill the chillies and pepper hard so they turn black. Transfer into a plastic bag with the salt and let them steam in their own heat. After 10–15 minutes, when they are cool enough to handle, remove the skin from the chillies and pepper by massaging them while they are still in the bag. Remove them from the bag and cut them lengthways. Remove the seeds but reserve these for the next step. Chop the fruit finely.

2 Heat a cast-iron pan on a medium heat. Toast the reserved chilli and pepper seeds together with the coriander, cumin and black peppercorns until everything turns golden brown and you can clearly smell the spices, around 2 minutes. Crush the spices coarsely using a pestle and mortar.

3 Heat a cast-iron pan on a medium-to-high heat and add the oil. Add the onion and garlic when it begins to smoke and fry for around 5 minutes while stirring. Add the chillies, pepper and tomato purée and leave to simmer for around 10 minutes while stirring. The mixture should be a dark colour and almost caramelised.

4 Transfer into a food processor together with the lemon juice, crushed spices and salt. Blend until smooth. Add a little more oil if it gets too thick. Store in a sterilised glass jar in the refrigerator. It will keep for at least 2 weeks.

MIDSUMMER'S LOUISIANA HOT SAUCE

500 g (1 lb 2 oz) red jalapeños

1 tablespoon rapeseed (canola) oil

2½ teaspoons sea salt flakes

2½ teaspoons water

100 ml (3½ fl oz/scant ½ cup) Champagne vinegar
    or white wine vinegar

1 Cut the tops off the jalapeños and remove the core. Set aside 100 g (3½ oz). Put the remaining 400 g (14 oz) in a bowl together with the oil. Then stir to ensure everything is coated.

2 Light the barbecue (grill) and while the fire is still burning grill the jalapeños hard so that the skins turn black. Set aside and leave to cool completely.

3 Place all the chillies, salt and water in a food processor and blend until smooth. Pour into a fermentation jar with a water trap and leave at room temperature for at least 6 weeks.

4 Press the mixture through a sieve (fine-mesh strainer). Add the vinegar and fill sterilised glass bottles. The sauce will keep in the refrigerator for several years.

SMOKIER SAUCE **If you want a little more of the smoky flavour, you can buy a burnt oak infusion spiral (medium strength) that you can put in the jar during step 3 of the fermentation process. They are available to buy from shops that sell brewing and wine making equipment.**

SMOKED ONIONS

500 g (1 lb 2 oz) onions, halved
1 garlic bulb, halved widthways
fresh mixed herbs, e.g. rosemary and thyme
peel of 1 unwaxed lemon
200 ml (7 fl oz/scant 1 cup) rapeseed (canola) oil
½ teaspoon salt
100–200 g (3½–7 oz) smoker chips

1   Light the barbecue (grill). Get a large baking tray (pan) and a smaller heatproof plate with a 1–1½ cm (½ in) high edge (the edge can't be higher than the one on the large baking tray). Place a thin layer of smoker chips in the bottom of the large baking tray then place the smaller plate in the tray.

2   Position the onions with the cut-side facing upwards together with the garlic, herbs and lemon peel on the smaller plate. Drizzle with oil and sprinkle with the salt. Cover with foil and place the baking tray with the plate on the grill while there are still flames. After a few minutes, the chips will begin to smoke and the smoke will seep out from under the foil (if the smoke doesn't seep out, you can unfold the foil a little at one corner to check it is smoking). Remove the baking tray from the grill when it begins to smoke and leave it to stand on the ground for a few minutes. Repeat this step three to four times. Remove the foil to check whether the onions and oil have taken on colour. Otherwise, repeat the procedure a few more times.

3   Place the onions in a sterilised glass jar, pour the oil over and seal the jar. If you like, you can fry the onions quickly in some oil just before serving – this will make the flavours blossom once again.

SMOKED TOMATOES

500 g (1 lb 2 oz) tomatoes
1 garlic bulb, halved widthways
fresh mixed herbs, e.g. rosemary and thyme
peel of 1 unwaxed lemon
200 ml (7 fl oz/scant 1 cup) rapeseed (canola) oil
½ teaspoon salt
100–200 g (3½–7 oz) smoker chips

1   Light the barbecue (grill). Get a large baking tray and a smaller heatproof plate with a 1–1½ cm (½ in) high edge (the edge can't be higher than the one on the large baking tray). Place a thin layer of smoker chips in the bottom of the large baking tray then place the smaller plate in the tray.

2   Position the tomatoes, garlic, herbs and grated lemon peel on the smaller plate. Drizzle with the oil and sprinkle with the salt. Cover with kitchen foil and place the baking tray with the plate on the grill while there are still flames. After a few minutes, the chips will begin to smoke and the smoke will seep out from under the foil (if the smoke doesn't seep out, you can unfold the foil a little at one corner to check it is smoking). Remove the baking tray from the grill when it begins to smoke and leave it to stand on the ground for a few minutes. Repeat this step three to four times. Remove the foil to check whether the tomatoes and oil have taken on colour. Otherwise, repeat the procedure a few more times.

3   Place the smoked tomatoes in a sterilised glass jar, pour the oil over and seal the jar. If you like, you can fry the tomatoes quickly in some oil just before serving – this will make the flavours blossom once again.

SMOKE WITHOUT FIRE **If you are unable to get hold of smoker chips, you can cheat to obtain that smoky flavour by sautéing onions or tomatoes in a frying pan with oil and a little liquid smoke.**

FERMENTED TREE ONIONS

250 g (9 oz) tree onions

200 ml (7 fl oz/scant 1 cup) water

10 g (2 teaspoons) salt, without iodine

2 tablespoons White Kimchi Base (optional),
    (page 200)

1 small root from a Chinese cabbage or white
    cabbage (20–30 g/¾–1 oz)

1 Remove the outermost layer from the tree onions then break off all the parts and place in a bowl.

2 Boil the water and add the salt. Stir thoroughly to ensure all the salt dissolves. Leave to cool then pour over the tree onions in the mixing bowl. Add the White Kimchi Base if you have it on hand – this is mostly acting as seasoning and you can get away with not using it.

3 Place the cabbage root in a 1 litre (34 fl oz/ 4 cups) sterilised clip-top preserving jar with a rubber seal (such as a Kilner jar) and add a few spoons of brine from the bowl containing the tree onions. Add the tree onions and press them down with a spoon. Pour in enough brine to cover, but leave 1–2 cm (½–¾ in) of air at the top. Fill a plastic bag with some water, knot the bag and add it on top as a weight. Close the lid and seal.

4 Place the jar on a plate and ideally stand it in a plastic bag since it is very likely that some liquid will seep out (don't seal the bag at the top). Leave at room temperature for 4–5 days.

5 Put the jar in the refrigerator and leave for at least 2 weeks so that the flavours have time to develop – the longer you leave it, the better it will taste.

WHISKY-PICKLED MUSTARD SEEDS

4 teaspoons mustard seeds, preferably a mixture
    of yellow and brown

100 ml (3½ fl oz/scant ½ cup) apple cider vinegar

90 g (3½ oz/scant ½ cup) cane sugar

100 ml (3½ fl oz/scant ½ cup) water

3 tablespoons whisky

1 teaspoon salt

1 Boil the mustard seeds in lightly salted water. Reduce the heat and simmer until the seeds are completely soft, around 40–60 minutes. Drain the liquid.

2 Boil the vinegar, sugar, water, whisky, salt and pre-boiled mustard seeds. Stir until the sugar has dissolved. Remove the saucepan from the heat and leave to cool.

3 Transfer everything to a sterilised glass jar and keep in the refrigerator.

FERMENTED GARLIC **Tree onions form in certain types of onion above ground. If you don't have access to tree onions, it's fine to use garlic instead. The principle is the same.**

QUICK-PICKLED BABY ONIONS

12 baby onions

1.5 litres (50 fl oz/6 cups) water

1 tablespoon salt

Syrup

100 ml (3½ fl oz/scant ½ cup) white wine vinegar

90 g (3½ oz/scant ½ cup) cane sugar

100 ml (3½ fl oz/scant ½ cup) water

2 teaspoons whole black peppercorns

2 teaspoons coriander seeds

1   Peel the onions and cut a cross into the top of each one. Boil the water and salt and add the onions. Boil for 8–10 minutes. Drain the onions and rinse until cold. Set aside.

2   To make the syrup, mix the vinegar, sugar, water, black peppercorns and coriander seeds in a saucepan and put on a medium heat. Bring to the boil and stir for around 2 minutes until the sugar has dissolved completely.

3   Put the onions in a sterilised glass jar and pour the hot syrup over them. Let them cool and then cover with the lid. Leave to stand in the refrigerator for at least 1 hour before using.

PICKLED WILD GARLIC CAPERS

1 kg (2 lb 4 oz) wild garlic capers

650 g (1 lb 7 oz/generous 2 cups) salt

300–400 ml (10–13 fl oz/1¼–generous 1½ cups) Champagne vinegar or white wine vinegar

1   Cut the capers off the fruiting head as best as possible to make it easier to use them when they are ready. Place the capers and salt in a glass jar and stir to ensure they are thoroughly mixed. Seal the jar and leave in a cool, dark place for at least 4 weeks.

2   Strain the capers and rinse the salt away using cold water. Take care to ensure you remove almost all the salt – the capers are already salty.

3   Put the wild garlic capers in a sterilised glass jar and fill with vinegar so that the capers are completely covered. Leave in the refrigerator for 1 week before using.

OVEN-BAKED ONIONS

Makes about 500 g (1 lb 2 oz/2 cups)

4 onions (about 600 g/1 lb 5 oz)
2 tablespoons butter
olive oil, for drizzling
sea salt and freshly ground black pepper

1   Preheat the oven to 200°C (400°F/Gas 6).
2   Peel the onions and cut them into quarters. Put them in an ovenproof dish, add the butter and drizzle the olive oil over them. Sprinkle with salt and pepper. Bake the onions in the middle of the oven for 20–30 minutes or until they have developed some colour – they can even be a little burnt. Take out and allow to cool before serving.

ROASTED PEPPER SEASONING

2 tablespoons coriander seeds
2 tablespoons Sichuan pepper
2 tablespoons whole black peppercorns

1   Heat a dry cast-iron pan over a medium heat. Toast the coriander seeds, Sichuan pepper and black peppercorns until the seeds start to go golden brown and there is a clear spice aroma.
2   Pound the spices in a mortar or mix them to a fine powder with a hand blender. Store in a jar.

ROASTED KALE

Serves around 8–10 as a side

500 g (1 lb 2 oz) kale or cavolo nero
4 small garlic cloves
100 ml (3½ fl oz/scant ½ cup) olive oil
sea salt and freshly ground black pepper

1   Preheat the oven to 120°C (250°F/Gas ½).
2   Cut off the stem of the kale if it is thick
    and woody (this can vary from one sort to
    another, and depending on maturity, but as a
    rule I remove it).
3   Put the kale leaves and garlic on a baking
    tray and drizzle oil over them. Sprinkle with
    salt and pepper. Roast in the middle of the
    oven for 20 minutes.
4   Take the roasted leaves out of the oven
    and transfer to a wire rack, with baking
    parchment underneath to catch any excess
    oil.

GRILLED AND STEAMED SPRING ONIONS

Enough for 6 burgers

100 ml (3½ fl oz/scant ½ cup) olive oil
sea salt and freshly ground black pepper
6 spring onions (scallions)

1　Pour the oil into a ziplock bag big enough to accommodate the spring onions. Sprinkle with salt and pepper. Put the bag next to the barbecue so it is close at hand.

2　Light the barbecue. Lay the spring onions on the grid while the charcoal is still actively flaming. Cook the onions all over so the surface gets a little burnt.

3　Using tongs, transfer the spring onions to the ziplock bag. Seal the bag and shake it so the oil covers all the onions. Leave them in the bag for about 20 minutes so they steam in their own heat.

DRY-ROASTED WALNUTS

Makes about 1 litre (34 fl oz/4 cups)

1 kg (2 lb 3 oz) walnuts with shells
　　(500 g/1 lb 2 oz without shells)
2 teaspoons mild chilli powder, e.g. piment
　　d'Espelette
sea salt

1　Crack open the walnuts and remove the shells.

2　Heat a dry frying pan (skillet), ideally a cast-iron one. Toast the nuts over a medium heat until they start to take on a little colour, for about 2 minutes. Shake the pan now and then so the nuts do not get too burnt, but don't worry if they burn slightly – it creates a good flavour.

3　Take the pan off the heat and season with chilli and salt.

NUT BUTTER

Several of the recipes in this book include nut butter – e.g. almond, cashew or hazelnut. You will find them in well-stocked shops, but be sure to only buy good-quality, natural versions – not the ones that have been sweetened with sugar. If you have a food processor with a knife blade at home, it is extremely easy to make your own nut butter. Mix the nuts at maximum speed until you have a fine, smooth butter. This will take 10–20 minutes, depending on food processor, type of nut and quantity. Initially, a nut flour will form, but the nuts will gradually start to release oil, creating a buttery consistency. It is a good idea to have a spatula to hand so you can scrape the nut mass down off the edges. If it is still dry after 15–20 minutes you can pour in a little extra oil, such as peanut, coconut or rapeseed oil (do not use cold-pressed oil – the flavour of the oil must be as plain as possible).

DEEP-FRIED SWEET POTATO CRISPS

Serves 6

4 large sweet potatoes
1 litre (34 fl oz/4 cups) peanut or deep-frying oil
sea salt

1 Cut the sweet potatoes into slices as thin as possible, ideally using a mandoline (you do not need to peel the potatoes).

2 Line a large bowl with a few layers of paper towel. Pour the oil into a high-sided saucepan and heat it to 180°C (355°F), then reduce the heat and try to keep the temperature at 180°C (355°F) as far as possible.

3 Deep-fry the sweet potato slices in the oil for 2–3 minutes, or until they are golden brown, turning them now and again using a slotted spoon.

4 Remove the sweet potato crisps (chips) and lay them in the paper towel-lined bowl so the excess fat is absorbed. Sprinkle with sea salt and turn them so that the salt is evenly distributed.

5 Serve as a snack or an accompaniment, or use them as a burger topping for extra crispiness.

DOUBLE-DEEP-FRIED CHIPS DUNKED IN CHEESE AND HERBS

Serves 6

800 g (1 lb 12 oz) firm potatoes (4-5 medium
    potatoes)
1 tablespoon pickling vinegar
1 tablespoon coarse sea salt
1–2 litres (34–68 fl oz/4–8 cups) peanut
    or deep-frying oil
chopped herbs, e.g. rosemary, thyme
    and parsley
50–75 g (2–2½ oz/½–⅔ cup) coarsely grated
    Västerbotten or other strong hard cheese

To serve
Tomato Ketchup (page 198)

Day 1

1 Cut the potatoes into 1 cm- (½ in-) thick
   sticks (you do not need to peel them first).

2 Put the potatoes in a saucepan containing
   plenty of water – about 2 litres (68 fl oz/
   8 cups) – and add the vinegar and salt. Bring
   to the boil, then boil for 5–10 minutes. Make
   sure the potatoes do not go too soft and fall
   apart – the cooking time can vary from one
   type of potato to another. Drain the potatoes
   and transfer them to a tea (dish) towel.

3 Pour the oil into a high-sided saucepan and
   heat to 200°C (390°F). Reduce the heat to
   medium and try to keep the temperature at
   200°C (390°F) as far as possible.

4 Deep-fry a third of the potato sticks at a time,
   for about 1 minute, while pushing them
   round with a slotted spoon.

5 Lift the chips (fries) out with a slotted spoon,
   transfer them to a metal colander and drain.
   Cool, cover with cling film (plastic wrap)
   and freeze overnight. (Save the oil for the
   next day.)

Day 2

1 Line a bowl with a few layers of paper towel.

2 In a high-sided saucepan, heat the oil from
   the day before to 200°C (390°F). Reduce
   the heat to medium and try to keep the
   temperature at 200°C (390°F) as far as
   possible.

3 Deep-fry the chips a third at a time for
   3–4 minutes, or until they are golden,
   turning them with a slotted spoon now and
   again. Put them into the paper towel-lined
   bowl so excess oil is absorbed. Sprinkle with
   sea salt and turn them over.

4 Remove the paper towel and sprinkle the
   herbs and cheese over the chips. Mix well and
   serve straight away.

WASH THE POTATOES **before peeling them (but do not scrub them so hard that
the peel completely disappears). Save the peel and try deep-frying it – the
thinner the peel, the better the flavour!**

DEEP-FRIED COURGETTE FLOWERS
stuffed with cream cheese and Parmesan

Serves 6

12 courgette (zucchini) flowers

120 g (4 oz/generous ¾ cup) plain
   (all-purpose) flour

1 teaspoon baking powder

½ teaspoon sea salt

1 egg

200 ml (7 fl oz/scant 1 cup) beer, lager
   or brown ale

1 litre (34 fl oz/4 cups) peanut or deep-frying oil

sea salt

Filling

120 g (4 oz/½ cup) cream cheese

2 tablespoon single (light) cream

2 tablespoon grated Parmesan

sea salt and freshly ground black pepper

1 Rinse the courgette flowers in cold water to get rid of all the dirt. Leave them on a tea (dish) towel to dry.

2 Mix the flour, baking powder and salt in a bowl. Whisk the egg in another bowl, then stir the whisked egg and beer into the flour mixture. Stir to form an even mixture.

3 Mix the cream cheese, cream and Parmesan together in a bowl. Season to taste. Put the cream cheese filling into a piping bag and pipe a little filling into each flower. Carefully fold the flower petals in so the filling does not run out.

4 Line a bowl with a few layers of paper towel and put it next to the cooker.

5 Heat the oil to 180°C (355°F) in a high-sided saucepan. Reduce the heat and try to keep the temperature at 180°C (355°F) as much as possible.

6 Dip the flowers in the flour and egg mixture and deep-fry 3–4 flowers at a time for about 2 minutes, or until they are golden brown. Push them around carefully with a slotted spoon now and again.

7 Lift the courgette flowers out and drain in the paper towel-lined bowl. Sprinkle with salt and turn them so the salt is evenly distributed. Serve straight away.

BARBECUED CORN ON THE COB with
garlic butter, crème fraîche and Parmesan

Serves 6

6 corn cobs with husks

2 garlic cloves

150 g (5 oz/generous ½ cup) butter,
    at room temperature

3 lemons

200 g (7 oz/generous ¾ cup) crème fraîche

3 thinly sliced jalapeños

sea salt

100 g (3½ oz/1 cup) grated Parmesan

1 Bring a large pan of lightly salted water to the boil.

2 Fold over the husks of the corn on the cob and remove the silk that lies between the husks and the kernels. Put the corn into the boiling water with the tips pointing downwards and boil for about 5 minutes. Take them out and fold the husks back again.

3 Light the barbecue. Barbecue the corn well all over while the barbecue is still actively flaming. If you want you can put the corn on the cob straight onto the burning charcoal – just make sure you use charcoal that has not been chemically treated. Barbecue the corn until the husks are almost completely black (they act as a protective casing around the corn kernels).

4 Take the corn on the cob from the barbecue and put to one side.

5 Peel and finely chop the garlic. Mix the butter and garlic with a fork in a bowl.

6 Rinse, dry and halve the lemons, and barbecue them with the cut surface facing downwards until they have developed a nice colour.

7 Remove the husks and put the corn onto a plate. Spread with garlic butter, drizzle over a little crème fraîche and sprinkle some sliced jalapeño on top. Add salt and grate Parmesan over them. Serve the corn on the cob together with the grilled lemon halves.

FENNEL, CARROT AND SAVOY CABBAGE COLESLAW

Serves 10

2–3 carrots (approx. 200 g/7 oz)

500 g (1 lb 2 oz) savoy cabbage

300 g (10½ oz) fennel

zest of 1 lemon + 2 tablespoons lemon juice

2 tablespoons finely chopped lovage or parsley

1 tablespoon Pickled Mustard Seeds (page 210)

lemon segments, to serve

Coleslaw dressing

2 teaspoons fennel seeds

1 teaspoon dill seeds

1 teaspoon black peppercorns

200 g (7 oz/generous ¾ cup) mayonnaise

2–3 tablespoons apple cider vinegar

½ teaspoon sea salt

1 For the coleslaw dressing, roast the fennel seeds, dill seeds and black peppercorns in a dry cast-iron pan over a medium heat until the seeds are golden brown. Pound the spices in a mortar or grind them to a fine powder in a spice mixer.

2 Put the spice mix in a bowl and pour in the rest of the ingredients for the coleslaw dressing. Whisk until fluffy.

3 Peel the carrots and trim the cabbage and fennel. Thinly slice the carrots, savoy cabbage and fennel, ideally using a mandoline. Transfer them to a bowl and pour the lemon juice over them. Knead well with your hands.

4 Stir in the dressing and top with the lemon zest, lovage or parsley and the pickled mustard seeds. Serve with the lemon segments.

KOHLRABI AND SWEETHEART CABBAGE COLESLAW

Serves 10

1 batch of Coleslaw Dressing
   (see recipe on the left)

400 g (14 oz) kohlrabi

500 g (1 lb 2 oz) sweetheart (hispi) cabbage

2–3 spring onions (scallions)

50 g (2 oz) horseradish

zest of 1 lemon + 2 tablespoons lemon juice

finely chopped dill

2 tablespoons olive oil

1 Make the dressing as described on the left.

2 Peel the kohlrabi and remove the coarse part of the cabbage and kohlrabi roots. Thinly slice the spring onions, kohlrabi and cabbage, ideally using a mandoline, then transfer the slices to a bowl.

3 Peel and finely grate the horseradish. Put the horseradish in the bowl with the cabbage and fennel. Mix in the lemon juice and knead well with your hands.

4 Fold in the dressing and top with the dill and lemon zest. Finish by drizzling the olive oil on top.

HANDY TO HAVE IN STOCK

Some of the ingredients in the book will not always be available at your regular corner shop. Pop into a well-stocked food shop or delicatessen and buy the following vital ingredients so you have them in your pantry the next time you feel like having a green barbecue.

Peanut oil

An oil that withstands really high temperatures, and a clear favourite for deep-frying. The oil itself is fairly flavourless, which means it will not compete with the flavours of other raw ingredients. There is, however, a cold-pressed version with a really clear peanut flavour. If you find it, use it as you see fit, but I recommend that you only add it as seasoning, as you would do with a really good olive oil.

Nut butter

Cashew nut butter, almond butter, hazelnut butter, peanut butter – incredibly easy to make yourself, keeps for a long time in the refrigerator, and absolutely wicked for flavouring your burgers with. Buy it ready-made or make your own (page 220).

Miso paste

The umami bomb! When I tried out miso paste as seasoning in the kimchi base instead of fish sauce it lifted the kimchi to a completely new level. Miso paste, in various forms, is sold in supermarkets as well as most Asian shops. I usually use an organic unpasteurised miso paste made of fermented grains and soy beans.

Vinegar

Malt vinegar, sherry vinegar and Champagne vinegar are my favourites. I use malt vinegar for full-bodied dishes, and like putting sherry vinegar in Asian-influenced dishes (it reminds me a bit of sake, with its sweet, nutty note). For quick-pickling, e.g. of jalapeños, Champagne vinegar is without peer.

Sichuan pepper

Available from well-stocked food shops, and has a flowery, citrusy, peppery flavour that is a bit chilli-like. Goes really well with coriander seeds and black pepper (page 132) and I like using it for seasoning grilled or fried vegetables.

Panko breadcrumbs

Japanese breadcrumbs that create a crispiness that regular breadcrumbs get nowhere near. Unbeatable for deep-frying and for giving your patties a good consistency and texture. Used frequently and almost shamelessly in the recipes in this book.

Piment d'Espelette (mild chilli powder)

Chilli from the village of Espelette in the Nive valley in the French Basque Country. Personally I find that as a dried chilli seasoning it is unbeatable. It is big on flavour and has an ideal mild heat – unlike ordinary chilli powder, which often has a slightly acrid, strong chilli sting, but less flavour. Piment d'Espelette is available in many delicatessens, but you can also buy it online.

Smoking wood chips

Available in most shops selling barbecues and barbecue accessories. I use Abu smoking wood chips, which are normally used for smoking fish, but they work at least as well for smoking other ingredients such as tomatoes (page 208). As the wood chips are so fine they create smoke faster than other wood chips.

Black rice

Despite the name, this isn't rice but a type of grass. It looks good, is tasty and rich in antioxidants. Available from larger supermarkets.

Black garlic

Still a little tricky to get hold of, but we will doubtless be seeing more of it in shops in future. It is a wonderful seasoning, and very different from ordinary garlic in its raw form. Mild and characterful, with a sweet toffee note, it has a consistency reminiscent of soft liquorice. You can also make black garlic yourself by wrapping garlic in cling film (plastic wrap) and leaving it in a food dehydrator set to 55°C (130°F) for three weeks.

Active charcoal powder

Sibylle's Bakery in Malmö, Sweden, sells a black loaf that I love, and this bread has formed the basis for the black charcoal buns in this book (page 194). The charcoal powder is above all for effect – the bread really does go jet black – but it also creates a lovely flavour, and Japanese tradition holds that it has purifying properties. I order my charcoal online through the Danish company Sort of Coal, which imports active charcoal made from charred pine needles from Japan.

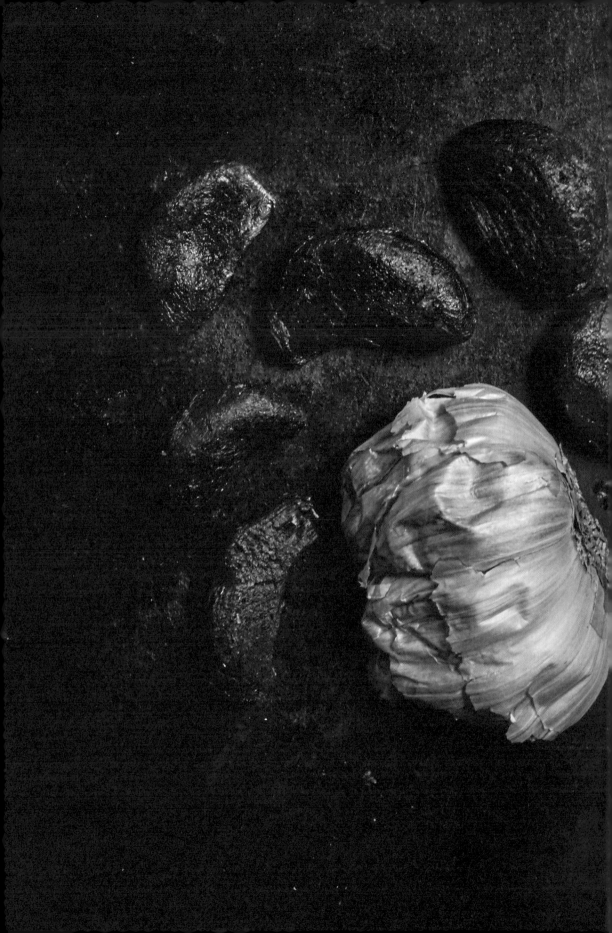

INDEX

THE GREEN BARBECUE COOKBOOK

THE GREEN BARBECUE COOKBOOK

Initially published in Swedish as Gröna Burgare
and Eld rök grönt by Bonnier Fakta, Stockholm
Published in the English language by arrangement
with Bonnier Rights, Stockholm, Sweden
Published in 2022 by Hardie Grant Books, an imprint
of Hardie Grant Publishing

Hardie Grant Books (London)
5th & 6th Floors
52–54 Southwark Street
London SE1 1UN

Hardie Grant Books (Melbourne)
Building 1, 658 Church Street
Richmond, Victoria 3121

hardiegrantbooks.com

Text © Martin Nordin
Food photography © Martin Nordin
Portrait and other photography © Oskar Falck

British Library Cataloguing-in-Publication Data.
A catalogue record for this book is available from
the British Library.

The Green Barbecue Cookbook
ISBN: 978-1-78488-547-2

10 9 8 7 6 5 4 3 2 1

Publishing Director: Kajal Mistry
Editor: Eila Purvis
Designer: Stuart Hardie
Proofreader: Emma Bastow
Indexer: Cathy Heath
Production Controller: Nikolaus Ginelli

Colour reproduction by p2d
Printed and bound in China by Leo Paper Products Ltd.

MIX
Paper from
responsible sources
FSC
www.fsc.org   FSC™ C020056